Daily Life and Demographics in Ancient Japan

Michigan Monograph Series in Japanese Studies
Number 63

Center for Japanese Studies
The University of Michigan

Daily Life and Demographics in Ancient Japan

William Wayne Farris

Center for Japanese Studies
The University of Michigan
Ann Arbor, 2009

*Open access edition funded by the National Endowment for the Humanities/
Andrew W. Mellon Foundation Humanities Open Book Program.*

Published by the Center for Japanese Studies,
The University of Michigan
1007 E. Huron St.
Ann Arbor, MI 48104-1690

Library of Congress Cataloging in Publication Data

Farris, William Wayne.
    Daily life and demographics in ancient Japan / William Wayne Farris.
        p. cm. — (Michigan monograph series in japanese studies ; no. 63)
    Includes bibliographical references and index.
    ISBN 978-1-929280-49-0 (cloth : alk. paper) — ISBN 978-1-929280-50-6
(pbk. : alk. paper)
        1. Japan—Population—History. 2. Japan—Social conditions—To 1600.
I. Title. II. Series.

HB3651.F368   2009
952'.01—dc22

                                                                            2008044108

This book was set in Palatino Macron.
Kanji set in Hiragino Mincho Pro W3.

Printed in the United States of America

ISBN 978-1-929280-49-0 (hardcover)
ISBN 978-1-929280-50-6 (paper)
ISBN 978-0-472-12800-6 (ebook)
ISBN 978-0-472-90196-8 (open access)

To Chong-mi

Contents

Illustrations

TABLES

Acknowledgments

This work came about as a necessary preliminary task to writing a book about Japanese medieval population. After completing the first installment of my research almost twenty years ago in *Population, Disease, and Land in Early Japan, 645-900,* I continued to collect data and interpretations bolstering my previous contentions. Since plunging into the writing of what eventually became *Japan's Medieval Population: Famine, Fertility, and Warfare in a Transformative Age,* the pace and scope of work on ancient demography both in Japan and the United States has picked up speed.

I would like to thank the Japan–U.S. Educational/Fulbright Commission and the Social Science Research Council for funding a year-long stay at Tokyo University in 1999. Special gratitude goes to professors Murai Shō-suke and Satō Makoto and the Scholars for a New Ancient History based in Tokyo. Thanks also go to Professor Tomobe Ken'ichi for sponsoring my visiting professorships at Keiō University in 2000 and 2003 and to Professor Hongō Kazuto for supporting my application to use the world-class facilities of Tokyo University's Historiographical Institute in 2001. The Northeast Asia Council of the Association for Asian Studies and the University of Tennessee provided financial support in that year. I especially appreciated the chance to talk to numerous scholars, including Kuroda Hideo, Amino Yoshihiko, Ishii Susumu, Tamura Noriyoshi, Kitō Hiroshi, and Saitō Osamu. I feel the deepest gratitude to Han Chong-mi, a Ph.D. candidate at Tokyo University's Division of Comparative Literature, who assisted this project in ways so diverse I cannot list them all.

Any mistakes, of course, are the responsibility of the author.

INTRODUCTION

Scholars have devoted considerable time and attention to the study of population in the ancient era (here defined as terminating in 1150 CE). Meiji scholar Yokoyama Yoshikiyo (1826–79) was probably the first, but he was eventually followed by the doyen of ancient demographic and quantitative history, Sawada Goichi (1861–1931), whose remarkable *Quantitative Research on Economics and Administration During the Nara Period* still defines research three-quarters of a century later.[1] Kitō Hiroshi, a demographer of the Edo period, has stimulated recent interest with two monographs, the first coming in 1983 and a revised version appearing in 2000.[2]

The energy applied to such a seemingly remote and difficult topic has not been wasted since even those who have not investigated ancient population have admitted its importance. For many, such as George Sansom and John Hall, it was the driving force behind the need for more food and the widespread land clearance that reputedly unleashed elite greed and undermined the Chinese-style state. For William McNeill, it was epidemic disease that caused population to stabilize or even decrease, thereby creating conditions in which a centralized, bureaucratic state could not long survive.[3]

This book attempts to synthesize previous work and analyze ancient population from several perspectives. To this end, it presents an historiographical overview of different figures, showing how they were computed as well as their strengths and weaknesses; makes estimates for the early eighth, mid-tenth, and mid-twelfth centuries; and then tries to evaluate those numbers in light of the relevant social and economic background. Critical variables include mortality parameters such as disease, famine, and war; factors indirectly indicating demographic trends and/or affecting fertility and longevity such as farming and agricultural technology; the labor market and industry; trade and the degree of urbanization; kinship, marriage, and the family; and commoner physical well-being as defined by everyday items (clothing, diet, sanitation, and housing).

The central argument will be that the population of ancient Japan (excluding Hokkaido and the Ryukyu chain) essentially remained static between 700 and 1150, with a decrease occurring around 950.[4] A major reason for this reversal of an earlier growth trend was the impact of pestilence, for

1

which I have gathered much more data than were available in 1985, when I first addressed this issue.[5] Famine and occasionally war exacerbated this shift. The drift toward lower population in the tenth and early eleventh centuries is readily visible in several areas: agriculture, where large tracts of land reverted to wilderness and peasants adapted technology to a lower worker-to-arable ratio; the labor market, where wages climbed and construction projects remained unfinished; industry, where labor-saving devices became common; and the demonetization of commerce and deurbanization of society. Only after 1050 did the population begin to recover to the level it had achieved in 700, as suggested indirectly by evidence from agriculture, trade, and cities. Hopefully, this essay will lead to new directions in research, even as it reinforces a well-known contention.

HISTORIOGRAPHICAL OVERVIEW

As is readily apparent from Table 1, there is no dearth of numbers purporting to represent Japan's total population at various times throughout the ancient era. It is equally obvious that most "estimates" derive from the Buddhist traditions of Shōtoku Taishi or the monk Gyōki and give modern scholars no idea about their method of calculation—if, indeed, they were computed at all. Leaving these aside, as well as the untenable numbers attributed to Inō Hidenori and the prewar Home Ministry (Naimushō chirikyoku), I shall concentrate on the figures proposed by prewar scholars Yokoyama Yoshiki-yo, Kimura Masakoto (1827–1913), and Sawada Goichi, and then proceed to examine postwar contributions. In evaluating the various estimates, I shall deal with three issues: the nature and validity of the sources, scholarly assumptions, and historical reasoning.

The first attempt to calculate Japan's ancient population occurred in 1879, when Yokoyama Yoshikiyo, a legal and literary scholar, computed three numbers for ninth- and tenth-century Japan. According to Yokoyama, Japan contained 3,694,331 persons in 823, a total he derived as follows. Utilizing an 823 regulation (kyaku) presumably denoting all allotment fields (kubunden) in Kyushu at that time (65,677 chō), he argued that the island contained 13.3 percent of all administrative villages according to the generally reliable tenth-century encyclopedia Wamyō shō.[6] A critical assumption was that each village throughout Japan had the same amount of kubunden. He then multiplied the number of chō in the 823 regulation by 7.5 (or divided by .133) to reach the total area of allotment fields in all Japan (492,557.5 chō). Thereupon, Yokoyama referred to household registers supposedly showing one chō supported 7.5 persons and multiplied to arrive at his total.

Even at a casual glance, the reader may note that this calculation has

Table 1. Pre-1945 Population Estimates for 589–1155

Date	Figure	Source
589	3,931,152	*Shōtoku taishi denki*-Q(S)
589	4,988,842	*Taishi den*-Q(S)
589	5,031,050	*Taishi den no shō*-Q(S)
610	4,969,000+	*Jugen ikō*; Nishikawa, *Ryōiki ninzu kō*; *Oritakushiba no ki*; *Ruijū meibutsu kō*; Suzuki, *Kōfu taii*-all Q(S)
610	4,990,000	*Jugen ikō*; Nishikawa, *Ryōiki ninzu kō*-both Q(S)
724–48	4,508,950	*Ruijū meibutsu kō*-Q(G)
724–48	4,584,893	*Gyōki daibosatsu gyōjōki*-Q/C
724–48	4,899,648	*Fusō koku no zu*-Q(G)
724–48	4,588,842	*Kairiku kōtei saiken ki*-Q(G)
724–48	5,000,000	*Gyōki shikimoku*-Q(G)
724–48	8,000,000+	*Jugen ikō*; Nishikawa, *Ryōiki ninzu kō*-Q(G)
724–48	8,631,000+	Nishikawa, *Chōnin no*; *Ruijū meibutsu kō*; *Oritakushiba no ki*; Suzuki, *Kōfu taii*-Q(G)
724–48	11,119,648	*Kairiku kōtei saiken ki*-Q(G)
724–48	6-7,000,000	Sawada
823	3,694,331	Yokoyama
859–922	3,762,000	Yokoyama
901–23	20,000,000	Inō, "Kokon kokō kō"
923	11,280,167	*Chiri kyoku zappō*; *Dai Nihon denseki kosū kakyū seki hikaku hyō*
947–1003	4,416,650	Yokoyama
969–984	4,416,650	Kimura, "Koseki no jinkō"
987–1011	22,083,225	Inō, "Kokon kokō kō"
1155	24-25,000,000	Inō, "Kokon kokō kō"

Source: Takahashi Bonsen, *Nihon jinkō shi no kenkyū*, 1:35–81.

Q refers to a figure that is quoted with no hint as to how it was tabulated.

Q(S) indicates that the figure is quoted (and not calculated) from folklore surrounding Shōtoku Taishi.

Q(G) means that the tally is quoted (and not computed) from legends about Gyōki. Note that three traditions seem to be associated with the Nara monk.

three serious drawbacks. First, Yokoyama believed that there were only 3,762 administrative villages in *Wamyō shō*, which results in a number that is too low. (There were in fact 4,041.) Second, and most fatally, it is unclear why he restricted his enumeration of fields merely to allotment paddies. There were numerous other kinds of arable, including newly cleared paddy and dry tillage, which should have been considered because people sustained themselves from these as well. This serious omission would also tend to lead to a figure that is too low. Third, his determination that one *chō* could support 7.5 persons is somewhat arbitrary, being based simply upon what household registers from northern Kyushu seemed to reveal. Other scholars, notably Takigawa Masajirō and Sawada Goichi, have argued for a much lower figure; if they are right, then Yokoyama's tabulation overestimates the population supported by *kubunden*.[7] For these reasons, Yokoyama's tabulation for 823 is most probably inaccurate.

For the years 859–922, Yokoyama inferred a figure of 3,762,000. He reached this number merely by taking what he thought was the total number of administrative villages (3,762) in *Wamyō shō*, multiplying the figure by 50 (the average number of households per village), and then by 20, the number he assumed lived in each household. This calculation also has several fatal flaws. Not only did Yokoyama miscalculate the number of administrative divisions in *Wamyō shō*, but his average of 1,000 persons per administrative village is too low, as shown by both Sawada in 1927 and Kamata Motokazu in 1984.[8]

The figure of approximately 4.4 million for 947–1003 comes from a passage in the "Japan chapter" *(riben zhuan)* of *The History of the Sung Dynasty (Sung shu)*. According to the section quoted by Yokoyama, the Tōdaiji monk Chōnen (938–1016) arrived at the Chinese court in 983 with several documents, among them *A Record of Kingly Eras (ōnendai ki)* that purported to enumerate the total number of administrative villages *(gō)*, post-stations *(eki)*, and most importantly taxable adults *(katei; 883,329)* in his native land.[9] Assuming that there were 5 such males per household, Yokoyama then tabulated the total number of households at 176,666. And because he believed, based on statements in Miyoshi Kiyoyuki's (847–918) early tenth-century *Twelve-Article Opinion Memorial (Iken jūnikajō)*, that each household then contained about 25 persons, he multiplied to obtain a figure just over 4.4 million.

Although this estimate does not present the prohibitive difficulties of the earlier ones, there are at least two grounds for suspicion. First, the documentary basis for total taxable males is unclear. *A Record of Kingly Eras*, known only through the Sung history, claimed to be authoritative as far back as mythological times. Since Chōnen never explained what sources were employed to compile *A Record*, we can only wonder how current the 883,329 number may have been. Second, Yokoyama did not elucidate the reason that his calculation applied to the fifty-six years from 947 to 1003, even though Chōnen's visit to the Chinese capital occurred in 983. To be sure, the entry for Japan in the "Eastern Barbarians" chapter of *The New History of the Tang Dynasty*, compiled around 1050, also describes imperial reigns briefly, but it makes no mention of Japan's population.[10] This computation, therefore, is certainly open to doubt, especially for any time after the late tenth century.

The late Edo-early Meiji academic also tried in the same article to tabulate the islands' population for the Kamakura era, arriving even more dubiously at 9.75 million.[11] Despite his misreading of many sources and questionable methods, however, Yokoyama's figures survived unquestioned for nearly a century. Irene Taeuber cited his estimates approvingly in her 1958 work, *The Population of Japan*.[12] Furthermore, in 1976 McNeill used Taeuber's (really Yokoyama's) numbers to support his thesis of population stasis caused by repeated cycles of pestilence.[13] Yokoyama's work, therefore, has more than a passing interest for demographers and historians today.

Kimura Masakoto provided another Meiji-era calculation meriting discussion. A scholar of the National Learning School *(kokugaku)*, Kimura also found Chōnen's tally in the *Sung History* to be of interest. Unlike Yokoyama, however, he was less exacting in his methodology and merely multiplied Chōnen's number of adult males (883,329) by 10 to account for all the disabled persons, women, slaves, aristocrats, and others omitted from the figure, arriving at a total of nearly 9 million. Kimura never gave any reason for employing this multiplier; he did not, for instance, utilize the household registers in the Shōsōin to corroborate his method. Painstaking work by Sawada and Kamata shows the proper multiplier to range between 4 and 5, reducing Kimura's number by half or more.[14]

Unlike Yokoyama's totals, which continued to be used for want of better choices, Sawada Goichi's 1927 estimate of 6–7 million for the Nara period is nearly universally accepted even today. Putting his training in statistics to good use, Sawada learned to decipher documents and laws from the eighth, ninth, and tenth centuries.[15] Although the original thesis was relegated to dusty shelves in Tokyo University's Faculty of Letters until the 1960s, Sawada's published work turned out to be the only solid research surviving from the prewar era. Along with Hayami Akira's calculation of 12.3 million for the year 1600, Sawada's estimate of 6–7 million for 750 would eventually be recognized as one of a pair of bookends bracketing the historical era before the survival of more reliable data.

Sawada used a whole host of historical materials to derive his total.

Referring to *The Ordinances of Kōnin* (*Kōnin shiki;* finished in 820), which listed total rice sheaves loaned in Mutsu Province, and to an 815 law enumerating taxable males for the same region, Sawada proceeded to compute the ratio of taxable males in Mutsu per 1,000 sheaves of rice. He then utilized that number (27.07 males) to calculate the sum of revenue-producing men for each province for which loan totals were available.[16] Then, availing himself of the most accurate household registers *(koseki)* from the early 700s, Sawada established the proportion of taxable males to the rest of the population, added the two together, and adduced a total rural commoner population of about 5.5 million for the eighth century. Combining this tally with estimates for urban dwellers in Nara, noncommoners (slaves, *nuhi*), and unregistered vagabonds *(furōnin)*, he inferred the 6–7 million figure.

Most impressively, Sawada was not satisfied with one method. He utilized local records from provinces (Suruga and Tōtōmi), regions (Kanto, Kyushu, and Kinai), and even lonely Tsushima and tiny Shima, all of which seemed to support his estimate. Still determined to bolster his conclusions, Sawada then cited a 747 edict indicating the desired number of taxable males in aristocratic "sustenance households" *(fuko)* and in the administrative villages where they resided. Using extant household registers, he calculated the population of an "average" village at about 1,400 persons and then multiplied by the total number of village units listed in the tenth-century *Wamyō shō*, once again arriving at his original estimate of 5.5 million commoners or 6–7 million in all.

Still, seen from today's perspective, Sawada's methods raise several questions.[17] On his basic technique of utilizing loan rice, we may of course wonder how representative conditions in a frontier province such as Mutsu were. Was the proportion of taxable adult males in Mutsu, for example, the same as in the more densely settled Kinai? Second, Sawada based his research upon several ninth-century records, such as the 815 law and *The Ordinances of Kōnin*, and even the tenth-century *Ordinances of Engi*. Could these sources be considered valid for the Nara period (710–84), too? When it came to the 747 edict, critics could always argue that sustenance households, since they supplied revenues to the aristocratic class, were populated with an unrepresentatively high number of tax-paying males, a proposition that could then ruin Sawada's entire line of reasoning.[18] His research remained an interesting but fanciful mental exercise until after World War II, most likely for want of other studies examining the family, village, and related topics.

Despite the advent of World War II, seminal research continued. Demographer Takahashi Bonsen compiled a comprehensive list of various estimates. (See Table 1.) Marxist scholars Ishimoda Shō and Tōma Seita argued that the households represented in the registers were patriarchal;

based upon Morgan's *Ancient Society* and Engel's *The Origin of the Family, Private Property, and the State*, they constructed a grand theory about the development of ancient society and the family. Their theory, called the "reality hypothesis" *(jittai setsu)*, assumed that households appearing in the Shōsōin documents indicated persons living under one roof and reflected a fair measure of social reality. During the 1950s and 1960s, Kishi Toshio began to punch holes in Ishimoda and Tōma's schema, arguing instead that households were legal fictions *(gisei setsu)*.[19]

This debate held center stage until the early 1970s. By that time, an archaeological boom was underway, and villages uncovered in excavations seemed to support Kishi—in other words, the small pit dwellings home to 2–8 persons did not correspond closely to the size of households recorded in the documents. They were too small to have coincided with the mammoth households (25–30 persons) in the registers. In 1972, Urata Akiko demonstrated that the ancient household was an artificial unit devised by the government to draft soldiers.[20] Census-takers merely combined dwelling units until they had obtained four or more healthy adult males, conscripting one to be a soldier. The resulting amalgamation of men and their families became an administrative fiction called a "household" *(ko)*. To be sure, such units were not entirely divorced from reality, but Urata's work pointed out the need for caution in using Nara population documents.

Archaeology supplied another piece of the puzzle in 1978. Koyama Shūzō, trained by J. Edward Kidder at International Christian University, devised a method for estimating Japan's population throughout the Jōmon epoch (10,500–900 BCE).[21] (See Table 2A.) Among Koyama's accomplishments were: (1) the development of the proposition that the Jōmon period comprised one complete demographic cycle, with a peak of about 262,000 in the middle Jōmon (ca. 3,500–2,400 BCE), falling to less than 100,000 by its end; and (2) the description of varying regional trends for eastern Honshu, western Honshu/Kyushu, and the Japan Sea littoral north of Kyoto. At about the same time, historical demographer Kobayashi Kazumasa of Kyoto University used the more than 5,000 skeletons excavated from the Jōmon age to compute life expectancies by gender: 34 years for males and 24 for women. Because Kobayashi had purposely omitted children's bones from his sample, when he made allowances for infant mortality, life expectancy at birth fell to a meager 16–17 years.[22] For the first time scholars had vital statistics for the ancient era, albeit the prehistoric Jōmon.

In 1983 Kitō Hiroshi, working at Sophia University, wrote a popular and seminal history of Japanese population *(Nihon nisen nen no jinkō shi)*.[23] Synthesizing almost all previous research, Kitō made the following two critical contributions to the study of ancient population. First, he retabulated

Table 2A. Kitō's Archipelago-wide* Estimates, 7,500 BCE–1150 (1983 version)

Period	Estimate
Initial Jōmon**	21,900
Early Jōmon**	106,000
Middle Jōmon**	262,500
Late Jōmon**	161,000
Yayoi**	601,500
750 CE	5,589,100
900	6,437,600
1150	6,916,900

Source: Kitō Hiroshi, *Nihon nisen nen no jinkō shi*, 12–13. Regional breakdowns are given in both this and the next table.
  *Excluding Hokkaido and the Ryukyu chain.
  **Kitō utilized Japanese archaeological periodization, which is based on the relative dating of ceramic styles. The use of absolute dates is eschewed. However, the numbers proffered here correspond roughly to the analogous dates given in Table 2B.

archipelago-wide and regional figures for the Yayoi through late Heian periods using his own new methods. (See Table 2A.) Second, he endorsed Koyama's idea of the demographic cycle, arguing that Japan had passed through two during prehistoric and ancient times. The earliest one was Koyama's Jōmon era; the second began with the Yayoi epoch (900 BCE–250 CE) and continued until at least the twelfth century, by which time it had reached its static phase.

Kitō's book raised many questions, but few were more important than those concerning the second cycle. It was clear enough that the agricultural and metallurgical revolutions occurring in the Yayoi period had initiated growth, but it was uncertain how long the expansion phase had lasted. Population had purportedly grown during the Yayoi and Tomb periods (250–650 CE), but Kitō never explained why or quantified the increase. Most significantly, when had the archipelago entered the static or declining stage of the second cycle? Kitō seemed to opt for the late eighth century, but he gave few reasons for his conclusion. In particular, this finding seemed to contradict the conventional wisdom that an expanding number of residents

Table 2B. Kitō's Estimates for Archipelago-wide* Population,
8100 BP–1150 (2000 version)

Period	Estimate
8100 BP	20,100
5200 BP	105,500
4300 BP	261,300
3300 BP	160,300
2900 BP	75,800
1800 BP	594,900
725	4,512,200
800	5,506,200
900	6,441,400
1150	6,836,900

Source: Kitō Hiroshi, *Jinkō kara yomu Nihon no rekishi*, 16–17.
*Excluding Hokkaido and the Ryukyu chain.

was converting more virgin territory into paddies and fields at that time.

The 1980s were a time of great productivity. In addition to Kitō, Dana Morris, also trained in Edo-period demography, analyzed Nara and Heian household registers and made some notable conclusions.[24] He argued that the average household was composed of eight to ten persons, primarily because of the prevalence of duolocal marriage patterns. These large families could retain adult labor more easily, resulting in a steadier supply overall. The big household was absolutely vital since peasant settlements were dispersed and unable to provide the communal services so essential to rice agriculture. Morris also asserted that the Nara-early Heian family bore a striking resemblance to the Tokugawa stem unit *(ie)*. Another contribution was his analysis of ninth- and tenth-century census records, in which he carefully traced for the first time in English how population registration operated in its failing years. The only drawback was his assumption, already disproved by Urata, that households listed in early eighth-century tax and census records were real dwelling units.

While Kitō and Morris were writing their essays, I was attempting to analyze the population data contained in eighth-century household and tax registers *(keichō)*. In the spring of 1979, at the suggestion of Susan Hanley, I took my data to Kobayashi Kazumasa at Kyoto University. Under his tutelage, and with the expert computer skills of oceanographer and erstwhile softball manager Harashima Akira, we managed to infer vital statistics for four sets of early eighth-century data. The method was similar to that applied to early modern materials and, like those villages, the cases fit best into the life tables of Model West, a variation constructed in part from modern Japanese census numbers.[25] (See Table 3.) Saitō Osamu, however, has raised some lingering doubts about these results.[26]

Another equally significant demographic discovery happened quite by accident. Through knowledge I had gained while studying with European medievalist David Herlihy and the good offices of Denis Twitchett, I became aware of William McNeill's *Plagues and Peoples*. As a world historian, McNeill had studied the nature of various infections and presented a chronology delineating the role of diseases in humanity's ancient past. Based upon an English translation of Fujikawa Yū's *A History of Disease in Japan (Nihon shippei shi)*, the most complete and authoritative source on Japanese pestilence, he argued the unconventional thesis that repeated plagues of foreign-borne "microparasites" had killed high percentages of residents and retarded demographic and economic growth from around 700 until the 1200s.

Studying the social and economic history of Nara and Heian Japan under Kishi Toshio had already convinced me of the critical role of infectious diseases in ancient Japan. After describing and analyzing the notorious smallpox epidemic of 735–37 and combining the insights gained thereby with other scattered data surviving from the ninth, tenth, and eleventh centuries, I endorsed McNeill's hypothesis. Within a year of the publication of my monograph *Population, Disease, and Land in Early Japan, 654-900*, Ann Jannetta brought new source materials and expertise to bear on the problem of premodern pestilence and concluded that the McNeill thesis had merit. Her conclusion, however, was tempered by her belief that most infections had become endemic to Japan earlier than either McNeill or I had argued.[27] Eventually, I assembled a more comprehensive list of all epidemics known before 1600 and described some of their ramifications on the society, politics, and economy.[28]

As research on the Nara and Heian periods was proceeding rapidly, anthropologist Hanihara Kazurō published a seminal article on a different aspect of ancient demography.[29] Utilizing Koyama's estimates for the Jōmon era and Sawada's for the 700s, and assuming a growth rate of 1 percent per annum for the millennial interval, Hanihara computed the rate of inmigration to the archipelago from Korea and the Asian continent. In all, he calculated that as many as 1.8 million persons had entered the islands from abroad during the Yayoi era (for Hanihara, 300 BCE–300 CE). Mark Hudson subsequently made detailed arguments to support this controversial thesis.[30]

10

Table 3. Vital Statistics for Four Early Japanese Populations

1. Mino Province in 702 a
Birth Rate = 51.21 persons b
Death Rate = 40.21 persons
Growth Rate = 11 persons
Life Expectancy at Birth = 27.75 years
Infant Mortality to Age 5 = 53.39 percent
Average Age at Death over Age 5 = 41.56 years

2. Hanyū Administrative Village in 702, females
Birth Rate = 50.47 persons
Death Rate = 36.47 persons
Growth Rate = 14 persons
Life Expectancy at Birth = 28.75 years
Infant Mortality to Age 5 = 55.48 percent
Average Age at Death over Age 5 = 40.57 years

3. Hanyū Administrative Village in 702, males
Birth Rate = 57.14 persons .
Death Rate = 35.14 persons
Growth Rate = 22 persons
Life Expectancy at Birth = 32.5 years
Infant Mortality to Age 5 = 61.69 percent
Average Age at Death over Age 5 = 38.86 years

4. Northern Kyushu in 702, males
Birth Rate = 54.34 persons
Death Rate = 37.34 persons
Growth Rate = 17 persons
Life Expectancy at Birth = 30.5 years
Infant Mortality to Age 5 = 59.16 percent
Average Age at Death over Age 5 = 40 years

Source: Farris, *Population, Disease, and Land*, 44.
    Note a: Adjustment of the Mino female birth rate to include all the population assumed that the sex ratio at birth was 100 females to 105 males.
    Note b: All figures are given per 1,000 population.

Hanihara's findings shed light on one of the critical reasons for Japan's demographic expansion in the first half of Kitō's second cycle, while at the same time undermining McNeill's contention that Japan's isolation had kept it safe from lethal epidemics until the late seventh century.

By the time Hanihara made his computations in 1987, more scholars were satisfied with Sawada's figure of 6–7 million for the Nara epoch, and there was a good reason for that posture.[31] In the early 1980s, archaeologists working in Ibaraki uncovered a cache of paper documents that had once served as lids for buckets of lacquer. Among the fragments so preserved was an official census report listing the commoner population for Hitachi Province in the late eighth century at about 192,000; when this number was adjusted to include servile and other groups, the total (224,000–244,000) was just a bit more than Sawada's calculation (217,000).[32] Now scholars had independent corroboration for Sawada's work. Today, it is the lone population tally accepted by almost all historians in Japan and the rest of the world, starting with the dean of Japanese demographers, Hayami Akira himself.

In 2000 Kitō rewrote his 1983 classic, integrating even more material and recalculating as he went. (See Table 2B.) While his figures were nearly the same, he added new estimates for 725 and 800, deleting his former reference to 750. This change was based on the work of Kamata Motokazu, about which I shall have more to say in Chapter 1. Also, for the first time in Japanese, Kitō recognized and endorsed the deadly effects of epidemics in producing the slowdown after 700.[33]

With the publication of Kitō's revised work, the ancient period was awash in numbers and theories. To be sure, Koyama had provided a widely accepted set of numbers for the Jōmon age and Hanihara and Kitō had made giant strides toward clarifying the nature and extent of the expansive phase until 700. Scholars from Yokoyama to Kitō, however, differed radically in their assessment of the rest of the ancient age, much less in the actual estimates they supported. Which were most acceptable in light of all that was known about the early period? Is it possible to derive more plausible figures for the eighth through mid-twelfth centuries?

NOTES

1. Yokoyama Yoshikiyo, "Honchō korai kokō kō," *Gakugei shirin* 5 (1879): 167–74. Sawada Goichi, *Nara chō jidai minsei keizai no sūteki kenkyū* (Kashiwa shobō, 1972).

2. Kitō Hiroshi, *Nihon nisen nen no jinkō shi* (PHP Paperbacks, 1983); *Jinkō kara yomu Nihon no rekishi* (Kōdansha, 2000).

3. George Sansom, *A History of Japan to 1334* (Stanford: Stanford University Press, 1958), 88; John Hall, *Government and Local Power in Japan, 500-1700* (Princeton:

Princeton University Press, 1966), 103; William McNeill, *Plagues and Peoples* (New York: Doubleday, 1976), 125.

4. I chose the epoch 700–1150 because (1) the year 700 comprises the beginning of the age when written sources are relatively plentiful; (2) there are arable figures for about 950 and 1150 for which scholars can compute, however dubiously, archipelago-wide population; and (3) analysis of these 450 years suggests that the basic demographic regime (birth and death rates, etc.) was similar. It should be noted that recently Sakaue Yasutoshi (*Nihon shi kenkyū* 536 [April 2007]: 1–19) has also come to the conclusion that the ancient age was a time of population stasis.

5. See William Wayne Farris, *Population, Disease, and Land in Early Japan, 645-900* (Council on East Asian Studies, Harvard University, 1985), 50–73.

6. For this order, see *Shintei zōho kokushi taikei, Ruijū sandai kyaku*, Kōnin 14/2/21 Remonstrance of the Council of State, 434–37.

7. Takigawa Masajirō, *Ritsuryō jidai no nōmin seikatsu* (Meichō fukyū kai, 1988), 111; Sawada, *Nara chō jidai*, 466–67.

8. Sawada, *Nara chō jidai*, 297–304; Kamata Motokazu, "Nihon kodai no jinkō ni tsuite," *Mokkan kenkyū* 6 (1984): 143.

9. *Chūgoku seishi Nihon den* 2 *Jiu Tang shu Wo guo riben zhuan, Sung shu riben zhuan, Yuan shi riben zhuan*, ed. Ishihara Michihiro (Iwanami bunko, 1986), 133–40.

10. Ibid., *Shin Tang shu dong yi zhuan riben*, 163–65. It should be noted that Yokoyama bolstered his computation by referring to similar figures, quoted but never explained, in two Edo works. See Takahashi Bonsen, *Nihon jinkō shi no kenkyū* (San'yū sha, 1941), 1:56.

11. For an evaluation of this figure, see William Wayne Farris, *Japan's Medieval Population: Famine, Fertility, and Warfare in a Transformative Age.* (Honolulu: University of Hawai'i Press, 2006), 2, 13.

12. Irene Taeuber, *The Population of Japan* (Princeton: Princeton University Press, 1958), 14.

13. McNeill, *Plagues and Peoples*, 126.

14. Sawada, *Nara chō jidai*, 74–75; Kamata, "Nihon kodai no jinkō," 143.

15. Sawada, *Nara chō jidai*, 143–310.

16. Figures for only 45 provinces survived in *The Ordinances of Kōnin;* all 66 can be found in *The Ordinances of Engi (Engi shiki),* dating from the early tenth century.

17. Kitō, *Nihon nisen nen no jinkō shi*, 45.

18. Kamata, "Nihon kodai no jinkō," 142.

19. For a much more detailed treatment of this debate, see Kishi Toshio, *Nihon kodai sekichō no kenkyū* (Hanawa shobō, 1973), 277–330.

20. Urata Akiko, "Henko sei no igi," *Shigaku zasshi* 81 (February 1972): 28–76. As will be clear from Chapter 3, the average size of the Nara or Heian commoner household remains a matter of debate. Some opt for the large household (*gōko*) of about 25–30 members, others for the smaller household (*bōko*). Both can be found in the households and tax registers of the Nara period, but Urata showed that both were administrative fictions. Archaeological remains suggest families of 2–8 members could live in a typical pit dwelling, but scholars have no way of knowing if a household constituted one or several pit dwellings. At the current level of research, uncertainties abound. Also see Chapter 3, Note 84, and William Wayne Farris, "Pieces in a Puzzle: The History of the Shōsōin Documents," *Monumenta Nipponica* 63 (winter 2008): 1–40.

21. Koyama Shūzō, *Jōmon jidai* (Chūō kōron, 1984), 10–40; "Jōmon Subsistence and Population," *Senri Ethnological Studies* 2 (1978): 1–65. It should be noted that some do not agree with Koyama's figures. See Serizawa Chōsuke, *Sekki jidai no Nihon* (Tsukiji shokan, 1960), 152; Gina Barnes, "Review of *Sacred Texts and Buried Treasures: Issues in the Historical Archaeology of Ancient Japan*," *Monumenta Nipponica* 54 (spring 1999): 124. Moreover, a current up-dating of Koyama's 1978 work would undoubtedly yield different figures. Finally, in 2003 a team of archaeologists led by Harunari Hideji suggested a new date for the beginning of the Yayoi period: 900 BCE. Their work was based on carbon found on Yayoi pots uncovered in Kyushu and has become widely accepted.

22. Kobayashi Kazumasa, "Jinkō jinruigaku," in Kobayashi Kazumasa, ed., *Jinruigaku kōza* 11 *Jinkō* (Yūzan kaku, 1979), 63–129.

23. Kitō Hiroshi later adjusted his figures somewhat in "'Chōsa' Meiji izen Nihon chiiki jinkō," *Jōchi keizai ronshū* 41 (March 1996): 65–79. Also see his more recent *Jinkō kara yomu Nihon no rekishi*, and below.

24. Dana Morris, "Peasant Economy in Early Japan, 650-950," PhD. diss., University of California at Berkeley, 1980, 65–105; "Land and Society," in Donald Shively and William McCullough, eds., *The Cambridge History of Japan* (Cambridge: Cambridge University Press, 1999), 2:194–99.

25. Farris, *Population, Disease, and Land*, 18–49. This study utilized Ansley Coale's and Paul Demeny's *Regional Model Life Tables and Stable Populations* (Princeton: Princeton University Press, 1966) , which condenses humanity's demographic experience into four models called North, South, East, and West. The first three are based on data deriving from northern, southern, and eastern Europe in the nineteenth and twentieth centuries. Model West is more diffuse, representing areas such as the United States, Great Britain, Taiwan, and Japan.

26. Saitō Osamu, "The Frequency of Famines as Demographic Correctives in the Japanese Past," *The Institute of Economic Research, Hitotsubashi University: Discussion Paper Series A* 386 (January 2000): 8, noted that several of the "failed" cases resulted from life expectancies less than twenty years, the lowest parameter in the Coale and Demeny life tables. Saitō has asserted that it is likely that eighth-century Japanese commoners may have lived on average "short, brutish, and nasty" lives of less than twenty years at birth. To be sure, the test cases that failed were also composed of the least reliable data, but in hindsight it would have been more prudent to have extrapolated the unexpectedly low life expectancies as well.

Despite the artificial quality of Nara "households," the vital statistics computed in 1979 seemed defensible for eighth-century populations, but it is possible, and perhaps even wise, to entertain doubts. First, unlike the analyses of Edo data, the work proceeded without knowing the overall rate of expansion. Holding both the growth rate and life expectancy (the two parameters in the Coale-Demeny life tables) as unknowns left a larger degree of uncertainty; statistically, it meant that the difference between one outcome and another was sometimes infinitesimal. Second, and more importantly, the birth rates were all unrealistically high. When I examined the documents for childless women, their number was much too large to maintain the tabulated birth rate of about 50 per 1,000 per year. If the birth rate was lower, then the growth rate would have been thereby reduced.

27. Ann Jannetta, *Epidemics and Mortality in Early Modern Japan* (Princeton: Princeton University Press, 1987), 16–32, 65–70, 114–17, 147–50. Jannetta, "Review Essay:

Historical Demography in East Asia," *Journal of Family History* 11 (winter 1986): 386, also suggests that epidemics prior to 735 were at least as lethal as the more famous smallpox outbreak that I described.

28. William Wayne Farris, "Diseases of the Premodern Period in Japan," in Kenneth F. Kiple, ed., *The Cambridge World History of Human Disease* (Cambridge: Cambridge University Press, 1993), 376–85.

29. Hanihara Kazurō, "Estimation of the Number of Early Migrants to Japan: A Simulative Study," *Journal of the Anthropological Society of Nippon* 95 (July 1987): 391–403.

30. Mark Hudson, *Ruins of Identity: Ethnogenesis in the Japanese Islands* (Honolulu: University of Hawai'i Press, 1999), 59–171.

31. Kamata, "Nihon kodai no jinkō," 131–41. The original document may be found in *Kanoko C iseki urushigami monjo: honbun hen* (Ibaraki-ken: Ibaraki-ken kyōiku zaidan, 1983), 105–10.

32. Kamata explains his adjustments in "Nihon kodai no jinkō," 133–41.

33. Kitō, *Jinkō kara yomu Nihon no rekishi,* 67–68.

CHAPTER 1

Population Estimates, 700–1150

When Sawada Goichi inferred a total of 6–7 million for Nara Japan, there was necessarily some question regarding precisely which years he meant. Because Sawada used materials from so many different centuries—household registers from 702, an edict from 747, *The Ordinances of Kōnin* from 820, and finally *The Ordinances of Engi* from 927, a historical demographer could be pardoned for wondering exactly to which era he believed this number best applied. When Sawada completed his work in 1927, this question may not have occurred to the author or his readers since deriving any statistic from such a distant epoch seemed like an amazing feat. In his conclusion to the chapter on population in *Quantitative Research on Economics and Administration during the Nara Period*, Sawada stated that the 6–7 million tally fit best for "the height of the Nara period," which he took to be the reign of Emperor Shōmu (724–49).[1] Later, Takahashi Bonsen concurred by referring to Sawada's estimate as belonging to Shōmu's tenure.[2]

Being desirous of greater precision even when there was none to be had, historical demographers have variously reinterpreted and retabulated Sawada's ground-breaking research. When in 1983 Kitō Hiroshi inferred a figure somewhat less than Sawada's, he argued that Sawada had exaggerated the unregistered populace, as well as the average size of the household (*ko*) and administrative village (*gō*), and then maintained that Japan's population in 750 was about 5.6 million. Yet Kitō was careful to leave himself "wiggle room" by stating that an estimate of 6 million for the Nara period would not be far wrong.[3]

Like most historians of the Nara era, Sawada had assumed that repeated governmental orders to create more rice fields, along with documentary evidence for these activities, meant that population was expanding throughout the eighth century. This assumption, however, left scholars in a bind. If Sawada's (or Kitō's) number best fit Shōmu's reign, and population was constantly growing as continuous land clearance seemingly indicated, then why were population totals derived from the ninth-century *Ordinances of Kōnin* or the tenth-century *Ordinances of Engi* somewhat less than Sawada's 6–7 million? Something appeared to be wrong.

Various attempts have been made to resolve this dilemma. One interpretation, chosen by Dana Morris and privately asserted by some Japanese historians, argues that Sawada's tally indeed applied to Shōmu's reign but that by 800 or 900 the population was even higher: 7–8 million in Morris' estimate.[4] If we follow this line of reasoning, then the numbers adduced from *The Ordinances of Kōnin* and *Engi* must have been out-of-date and therefore unreflective of the demographic and economic conditions of their respective times. Viewed over the long-term, however, this solution has a greater weakness: It leaves even less room for population gain during the late Heian and medieval eras, when most scholars agree that agriculture was advancing along with the rest of the economy.

In 1984 Kamata Motokazu of Kyoto University proposed a different answer to the Sawada quandary by critiquing one of the statistician's central arguments and reinterpreting Sawada's source.[5] Referring to the 747 edict attempting to bolster payments to aristocrats from their "sustenance households," Kamata argued that the figure listed in the order, "5 or 6 taxable adult males" (called *seitei*, aged 21–60) per household, was much higher than the legal norm.[6] The Kyoto scholar then pointed out that the usual criterion, both for conscription and tax purposes, was a mere 4 adult males per household.[7] The 747 edict had probably ordered a higher tally to succor the aristocracy, which at the time was having trouble collecting enough revenue to support its luxurious lifestyle.

Using the most reliable census records from the first quarter of the 700s, Kamata computed his own total for Japan's population around that time. Legally speaking, he pointed out, each administrative village was supposed to have at least 200 taxable men (50 households X 4 adult males). Because the rule of 4 taxable men per household was a legal fiction combining healthy adults paying full revenues with disabled or sick ones sending in partial dues, the precise figure came to 209, according to extant reliable census records. Assuming this standard to be applicable throughout all regions under government control, Kamata utilized the age structure and sex ratio reflected in credible household and tax registers to compute the requisite number of taxable teenaged males (17–20) at 39 and then established the legally mandated size of an administrative village at 1,052. As Kamata noted, this total was 348 fewer than Sawada's figure; multiplying 1,052 by the 4,041 administrative villages listed in the tenth-century *Wamyō shō*, he arrived at a rural commoner population of 4,251,132. When he factored in slaves, Nara urbanites, and unregistered people, Kamata's revised computation was about 4.5–5 million people for early eighth-century Japan.

The significance of Kamata's accomplishment should not be understated. He had "solved" Sawada's dilemma by devising a new, lower population figure for the period 700–750. The Sawada tabulation, Kamata argued, was most reasonable for the archipelago around 800; he drew further support from the proposed date of the lacquer documents: the Enryaku era (782–805). Recall that the figure for Hitachi Province dovetails nicely with Sawada's estimate, implying that his number was most applicable to the year 800. By Kamata's reasoning, a population of 4.5–5 million around 725 had grown to 6–7 million by 800, thus tying demographic increase to land clearance activities. What is more, Kamata believed that his own figure for 725 was based "on the administrative documents of practice," unlike those of his predecessors. Upon reading Kamata's article, Kitō immediately discarded his former calculations for 750 and recomputed, employing 4.5 million for 725 and 5.5 for 800.[8] (See Table 2A and B.)

Ingenious as Kamata's solution may seem, however, his reasoning is flawed. Given legal standards of 4 adult males per household and 200 per administrative village, he could indeed utilize the more reliable census records of the years 700–725 to flesh out the abstraction a bit, surmise a tally for the standard administrative village, and then infer an archipelago-wide total of 4.5 million by using *Wamyō shō*. But Kamata's method leaves scholars with the question: Was the Nara court so powerful that it could enforce a single legalistic yardstick for households and villages throughout the archipelago? Later premodern Japanese history attests to the vitality and stubbornness of regional variation; it is difficult to believe that the 700s were the exception, even though a "one-size-fits-all" legal source *(ritsuryō)* survives from that era.

Moreover, it can be argued that Kamata confused the concept of legal minimum with numerical average. If we follow his reasoning, it is hard to believe that the court would have permitted administrative villages smaller than 1,052 persons—the number of taxable men would have been too few and revenues too paltry. Units could certainly be larger than this, however; the 747 edict was addressing just such a problem by ordering that sustenance households contain 5 or 6 taxable men to profit high-born aristocrats. Kamata really calculated the archipelago's legally minimal population given the court's tax goals.

Indeed, in the one case where it is possible to confirm the population of an administrative village, Kamata comes out badly. A lone near-perfect household register, dating to 702 and showing 54 households for Hanyū Village in the Kamo District of Mino, survives in the Shōsōin. According to Kishi Toshio, the record had space for 4 more units, bringing its total to 58.[9] Assuming that the remaining 4 households averaged the same size as the others, the population of Hanyū Village would have been 1,206 persons, about 14.6 percent larger than Kamata's 1,052. When we multiply the higher tally by *Wamyō shō*'s 4,041 administrative villages, the result is 5.2–5.8 million, totals not so very different from Sawada's. Even more disadvantageous for Kamata, Mino administrative villages tended to be smaller than the archipelago average.[10]

In fact, where Kamata applied one legal standard for the topographically variegated Japanese islands, Sawada was careful to recognize regional diversity. In a later section of his book, Sawada computed the mean size of an administrative village for every province and then correlated his results with a province-by-province list of cultivated lands, also found in *Wamyō shō*.[11] (See Table 4.) Administrative villages evinced a range of populations, from less than 800 for small or isolated provinces such as Oki and Satsuma, to over 1,900 for densely settled areas such as Iga, Echizen, and Bizen. To be sure, Kamata would protest that Sawada's data originated from the ninth and tenth centuries (when, according to Kamata, the population grew), but it is hard to believe that regional variation was not also pronounced in the early 700s. In sum, Sawada's allowance for localism is much more convincing than Kamata's juridically derived computation with one standard fitting all areas.

Given the legalistic nature of Kamata's argument, the testimony from the Mino register, and the regional variation inherent in Sawada's original estimate, the latter's work still seems to merit acceptance. To what era does Sawada's work best apply? The following answer seems to be most appropriate. According to *Fragments from the Penal Statutes (Rissho zanpen)*, a reliable commentary on the Taihō criminal statutes of 701, the archipelago contained 4,012 administrative villages between 715 and 739.[12] The early provenance of this total is clear from the term used for the units *(gōri)*, applied during those few decades only. This source, rather than the mid-tenth century *Wamyō shō*, is more reflective of conditions in the early 700s and should have been employed by both Sawada and Kamata.

If we multiply 4,012 by the median value (1,400) Sawada computed for villages throughout the archipelago, the total registered rural commoner population equals 5,616,800. If we utilize 1,250, an average of Sawada's and Kamata's computations (also endorsed by Kitō), the total falls to just over 5 million. When allowances are made for slaves (about 10 percent, according to extant household and tax registers), urbanites (maybe 150,000 including Nara, Naniwa, and Dazaifu), and undetected individuals (100,000, averaged from Sawada), Japan's population between 715 and 739 falls within a range of 5.8–6.4 million.[13] This figure corresponds relatively closely to Sawada's original estimate. In other words, utilizing a source contemporary to the early eighth century and two different village averages combining the insights of all three scholars, Sawada's 1927 calculation still appears to be near the mark and applies best to the years 715–39.

The Mid-Tenth Century

A further problem remains, however. How do scholars interpret the data from the ninth-century *Ordinances of Kōnin* and the tenth-century *Ordinances of Engi*, which imply a static population of about 5–5.6 million? (See Table 5.) The first alternative is that these sets of data truly reflect the social conditions of their respective ages and that, despite regional fluctuations, the overall population of the archipelago remained about the same during the 800s and early 900s. The variations—sometimes sizable—in forty-five provincial and regional populations recorded in the 820 and 927 compendia bolster this notion. For example, Kyushu gained people while the population of the Japan Sea littoral west of Kyoto shrank. These differences in local data tend to corroborate the reliability of the two compilations by suggesting repeated surveying and re-copying in the ninth and tenth centuries.

Second, we might contend that both ordinances were inaccurate and the population was much greater than the data state. In this view, as peasants absconded from their overcrowded lands into the hands of a greedy elite, the census and land systems fell into desuetude and recorded population and tax receipts consequently dwindled. In turn, numerous aristocrats and religious institutions created estates *(shōen)* that went unnoted, for the most part, in government documents.[14] This hypothesis, favored by some Japanese and still preferred by many American scholars, is basically the same as Morris' solution to Sawada's dilemma, which, as described above, has several loopholes, among them the lack of corroborative evidence and less room for population expansion during the more prosperous medieval era.

A third interpretation—that real population was considerably less than the compendia show—is another option. To wit, the relationship between census and land systems on the one hand and population and government revenues on the other may have differed from that posited above. First, population and tax receipts declined in the face of higher mortality from disease and famine; then the census and land systems became moribund. *The Ordinances of Engi* lend some credence to this view since they contain about 20,000 fewer individuals than the ninth-century legal work. The elite was either unable or unwilling to secure new figures and maintained the old ones on the books (with some variations) despite a certain irrelevance to social reality. By holding onto the old eighth-century statistics, the elite asserted its right to larger revenues despite the reality of demographic loss. This hypothesis makes sense since institutionally the ninth century tells a tale of rulers' growing inability to make the Chinese-style system function as intended until the emergence of a new state structure *(ōchō kokka)* around 900.

The three alternatives described for the period between about 800 and 950 run the gamut from growth to decline. Can figures for Japan in the mid-tenth century help uncover what was really happening? In my view, scholars have espoused two reasonable methods of doing so at present, one by Yokoyama Yoshikiyo and the other by Kitō. Yokoyama's calculation, it will be recalled, relied upon the number of taxable adult males (883,329) reported by the Tōdaiji monk Chōnen in *The History of the Sung Dynasty*. Dividing this figure by the average tally of taxable men per household (5), Yokoyama arrived at a total of 176,666 households, which, he argued, contained 25 persons each. Yokoyama's estimate for the archipelago's population equaled about 4.4 million.

This computation includes no outrageous assumptions. Moreover, the reader will recall that Kimura Masakoto also used Chōnen's figure for taxable adults but merely multiplied 883,329 by 10 to account for the rest of the population. As noted earlier, when we utilize ratios derived from extant household registers, the multiplier falls to a value between 4 and 5. Kimura's estimate then shrinks to about 3.9–4.4 million, near Yokoyama's original number. These figures could well occupy the lower range of estimates for the mid-tenth century.

In 1983 Kitō devised another method utilizing completely different source material. It is well known that *Wamyō shō*, an encyclopedia compiled between 931 and 938 by Minamoto Shitagō (911–83), reports not just the total number of Japan's administrative villages, but also lists the acreage in rice fields at about 862,000 *chō*.[15] Arguing from eighth-century laws on the land allocation system *(handen sei)*, Kitō proposed that it took about 1.6 *tan* (or .16 *chō*) of wet-rice paddy to support the average grantee, yielding 5,375,000 persons. From the most reliable household registers Kitō also reasoned that about 16 percent of the population (860,000) would have been younger than 6 years, the minimum age to receive an allotment. Adding 250,000 for Heian's urbanites, Kitō arrived at a figure of 6,437,600 for early tenth-century Japan.[16] When he recalculated in 2000, he inferred a minutely higher total (6,441,400) by adjusting his method slightly.[17]

As Kitō readily admitted, he based his method on several big assumptions. He was primarily concerned about applying the strictures of an eighth-century land system to 900, but given the continuities in agricultural technology and land use over those two hundred years, this seems the least of his worries.[18] Rather, Kitō addressed at least four other crucial questions inadequately or not at all. First, *Wamyō shō* notes only paddy land for each province; as Amino Yoshihiko and others have been at pains to assert repeatedly, some substantial percentage of the rural population was engaged in livelihoods such as fishing, hunting, swidden cropping, and logging—that is, they were not all rice farmers.[19] Except for adding in Heian's occupants (250,000 in 1983; later 120,000), Kitō made no allowance for the diversity of early Japanese occupations.[20]

There is a rejoinder to this argument, however, made by no less than Amino himself.[21] He asserted that even though most peasants did not even consume rice daily, the various governments of Japan, from the Nara court to the Edo shogunate, calculated all economic activity in terms of its market value in rice. In other words, rice was the chief unit of accounting, despite its perishability. Therefore, because figures for total rice fields such as one sees in *Wamyō shō* may already embrace the relative value of all other productive activities as measured in the government's unit of account—rice or, in this case, rice fields—the whole rural population, including those subsisting by sundry occupations, is already included. Kitō would undoubtedly argue that this was the case for *Wamyō shō*, too.[22]

A second tricky part is converting paddy land into persons because it raises a critical question: Just how much rice land did it take to support one person? What does it mean "to support a person?" Should we include items used in barter or paid as revenue in the estimate? Kitō used an average of rice fields allotted to men and women according to the Nara-early Heian Chinese-style system of land tenure that presumed it required 1.6 *tan* to sustain the average person. On that basis he obtained a population of about 5.4 million. Unknown to Kitō, however, prewar scholars Takigawa Masajirō and Sawada Goichi had already debated this proposition at length.[23] They concluded independently that an average allotment of 1.6 *tan* was sufficient to support only about 60 percent (Takigawa) or 67–75 percent (Sawada) of a commoner's daily needs, excluding the land tax. Combining Kitō's, Takigawa's, and Sawada's estimates, I arrived at a figure of about 2.17 *tan* of rice land necessary to sustain the average person, and I shall utilize that number in the calculations undertaken below.[24]

The third and fourth difficulties apply only if *Wamyō shō*'s numbers represent actual cultivation conditions and not rice fields as a unit of accounting. As Philip Brown has shown for Kaga domain in the late sixteenth and seventeenth centuries, premodern methods of land measurement were often inaccurate.[25] How precise were the totals listed in Minamoto's tenth-century encyclopedia? According to Sakamoto Shōzō, the leading authority on local government and taxation in the mid-Heian era, provincial governors and their staffs were legally required to make a circuit of their jurisdictions once in their four-year terms to note agricultural conditions. They then compared survey results with records from previous tenures, especially with the famous "four authenticated maps" (*shi shōzu*) dating from the mid- and late eighth century.[26] Presumably, Minamoto relied on such information when he wrote out his province-by-province totals. Even though doubts persist, it is no simple matter to correct for such possible mismeasurement without several sets of independent province-wide surveys, none of which are extant.

Finally, all Japanese historians are aware that there were many tracts of uncultivated or abandoned fields by the 900s; the near-total disappearance of cultivators at the early estates *(shoki shōen)* that consumed so much of the court's and local notables' investment wealth in the late 700s is but one example.[27] Accordingly, most historians now submit that on average between 20 and 30 percent of arable had gone out of cultivation either permanently or temporarily by the middle Heian period.[28] Archaeologists are also now discovering that fields cultivated in the Nara age went to waste in later centuries.[29] The figures listed in *Wamyō shō* may well have encompassed a similar percentage of barren fields.

Given these serious questions, it would be most reassuring if some other source material were available for computing the population around 950. Unfortunately, at present there is no other material from which to estimate, however tenuously, a figure for 950. It seems reasonable, therefore, to recompute Kitō's total, assuming that the acreages in *Wamyō shō* represent a unit of accounting for all economic activity and then inferring that the figures describe actual cultivation conditions. In the first method, I divided the 862,806 *chō* noted in *Wamyō shō* by the amount of rice paddy necessary to support a person (.217), arriving at 3,976,065 persons. To this subtotal, I added 16 percent (636,170) to include infants aged 5 and below because that proportion is the only precise number available for the ancient period and there is little reason to expect significant divergence from the 700s. I also added another 150,000 for urban residents (100,000 in Heian), yielding a grand total of 4,762,235.[30] Even compensating for difficult-to-quantify categories such as undetected persons (100,000) and slaves (500,000), it seems unlikely that Japan had as many as 5.6 million inhabitants in 950.

The second method, which treats the provincial totals for rice fields as if they portrayed actual farming conditions and meets most, if not all, of the objections listed above, would work as follows. From the 862,806 *chō* listed in *Wamyō shō*, I subtracted 25 percent to account for abandoned land, leaving 647,105 *chō* being regularly farmed as rice fields. To be sure, this figure is an average, but given the estimates proposed by Toda Yoshimi, it may even be somewhat conservative. I then proceeded as with the first method, dividing the total rice acreage (647,105 *chō*) by .217 and further multiplying that total by 1.16 to account for nongrantees. The total population dependent upon rice comes to 3,459,179, a figure considerably smaller than Kitō's.

Estimating the number of rural folk who obtained their sustenance from livelihoods other than rice farming is fraught with unknowns. Many years before this became a serious issue, Hayami Akira posited that during the early Edo period about 10 percent of the countryside's populace was engaged in pursuits other than rice farming.[31] It is hard to believe that the figure would have been any lower for the mid-tenth century; if anything, we would expect that many more people lived by hunting, fishing, gathering, swidden, and other types of dry cropping. Various sources indicate that dry farming alone accounted for 20–25 percent of rural production in the 700s; by the early Meiji period it was over 60.[32] If we utilize a multiplier of 1.4, seemingly about right given the paltry evidence available, then the total rural population around 950 was 4,842,851.[33] Adding another 150,000 for urban residents, I arrived at a total of about 5 million. Again Japan's total population seems to have been no more than 5.6 million.

Table 5 provides a province-by-province comparison of the populations computed according to Sawada's rice loan method (927) and the second formula using the figures for rice fields in *Wamyō shō* (935) as explained above. Of Japan's sixty-six provinces, only about twenty come close to matching according to both modes of calculation. Most difficulties undoubtedly arise from the "one-size-fits-all" nature of each method: The "truth" lies somewhere in between. For instance, in Hida, Shinano, Mutsu, Dewa, and Ōmi, where the amount of rice acreage was recorded as high, figuring the population on the basis of land area probably leads to overestimation. In other cases, such as western Japan, it appears that the land was more densely utilized—or alternative occupations were more popular—than the model I devised would predict. Still, given the difficulties of inferring population by either method, the overall results are reasonably close.

Thus for the mid-tenth century I obtained estimates ranging from Yokoyama's minimum of 4.4 to a maximum of about 5.6 million persons. No matter which tally the reader chooses or even if he opts for the figure calculated by Sawada from data listed in *The Ordinances of Engi* (5.0–5.6 million), they extend from somewhat to considerably smaller than the 5.8–6.4 million computed for the first decades of the eighth century. What social and economic factors help to explain the late ancient population trend?

A POPULATION ESTIMATE FOR 1150

In 1983 Kitō broke more new ground by inferring a population of 6,916,900 for 1150.[34] Although the method was borrowed from his research on the tenth century, the historical source was new. To obtain his figure, Kitō relied on a fourteenth-century encyclopedia entitled *Shūgai shō*; as he rightly observed, his late colleague at Sophia University, the eminent Nara-Heian social and economic historian Iyanaga Teizō, had studied many sources purporting to list Japan's total rice acreage for the ancient and medieval eras, and he concluded that *Shūgai shō* really employed numbers applicable to the late Heian period.[35]

Believing that the total paddy land noted in *Shūgai shō* was about 926,000 *chō*, Kitō then revisited the method applied to the contents of the tenth-century land register. Arguing from eighth-century laws on the land allocation system, he assumed that it took about 1.6 *tan* to support the average grantee, arriving at a figure of 5,787,500. Since according to the most reliable household registers, about 16 percent of the population would have been younger than six years, the minimum age to receive an allotment, Kitō then added that subtotal to make 6,713,500. Adding an indeterminate number for Heian's urbanites, Kitō arrived at a figure of 6,916,900 for mid-twelfth century Japan.[36] When he recalculated in 2000, Kitō reduced the figure for the inhabitants of Heian and argued for a slightly lower total of 6,836,900.[37]

The same objections can be raised against this method that cropped up for his work to estimate a population in 900. First, there is no telling whether *Shūgai shō's* areas were meant to reflect the economic activities of all country folk—or only rice farmers.[38] Second, it is doubtful that it required only 1.6 *tan* to sustain an individual even in 1150. Third, there is similar reason to wonder how accurately fields were measured, although governors and surveyors apparently made their appointed rounds and redacted three types of cadasters as late as 1150.[39] There is no documentation, however, to corroborate *Shūgai shō's* totals independently. Finally, according to Toda Yoshimi and others, large tracts of fields remained uncultivated, even as late as 1300; the twelfth-century land register may well have included many such lands.[40]

In particular, some would take issue with the second statement that more than 1.6 *tan* was necessary to support a person in 1150. Should the number not be considerably lower, thus increasing the estimate for the rice-farming populace? Some historians believe that late Heian agriculture performed markedly better than its predecessor, an interpretation subsumed under the rubric of the "age of widespread land clearance" and voiced by highly respected scholars such as Toda Yoshimi and Kimura Shigemitsu. They would raise the query: Even as more rice fields became productive, would not per-unit yield have risen as well?

I will deal with the topic of late Heian rice farming in Chapter 3. In general, little new research has appeared since the 1980s to bolster the argument for "an age of widespread land clearance" or more productive late Heian agriculture. Regarding yield per unit, Kitō's figure of 1.6 *tan* needed to support a person is by far the lowest figure yet employed for rice farming in 1150. To my way of thinking, Ishii Susumu was correct when he stated that yields in 1150 were not much better than in 750; dramatic improvements in Japanese agriculture did not take place until after 1300.[41] In converting rice paddy area to sustainable persons, it seems more reasonable to employ a divisor of 1.975 *tan*, a modest reduction from the 2.17 divisor used in computing mid-tenth century population and in line with Ishii's view and other evidence suggesting a modest increase in harvest per unit.[42]

Let us compute a range of population figures for 1150 using the only reliable source *(Shūgai shō)*, reprising the two formulas taking into consideration most, if not all, of the objections raised against Kitō's system. Initially, let it be noted that the total paddy land listed in the twelfth-century source was more than Kitō believed, equaling 956,558 *chō*. (See Table 5.) Assuming that this number represents a unit of accounting for all rural economic activity, I divided by .1975 to arrive at 4,843,332. Adding 16 percent, the only precise figure available for the ancient period, to represent infants yields 5,618,265 for the total rural population. No one knows for sure how many urbanites existed in 1150, but 200,000 (100,000 for Kyoto and another 100,000 for the various cities listed in Chapter 3) reflects the impression of increased urbanization in late Heian Japan.[43] The overall estimate for the Japanese archipelago is about 5.8 million; given the numerous imponderables in these equations, it seems most prudent to employ a range of 5.5–6.1 million persons, as calculated according to the first method.

The second formula assumes that figures for rice paddies portray actual cultivation conditions. Positing that only about 75 percent of these fields were actually under cultivation, I obtained an area of 717,419 *chō* regularly harvested by peasants. This converts to a population of 3,632,501 using the .1975 divisor; including children, the subtotal comes to 4,213,702. This number represents only the population surviving by wet-rice farming; in factoring in those living by alternative occupations, I multiplied by 1.4, again based on earlier reasoning. The total rural population is then 5,899,182, and adding 200,000 for urbanites as above, I arrived at about 6.1 million for the entire archipelago. Because of the uncertainties in this calculation, it seems wise to posit a range of 5.9–6.3 million for 1150.[44] (See Table 5.)

Breaking the archipelago's population down by region for the era 820–1150 reveals some interesting local trends beneath these island-wide figures. (See Table 6.) First, while there are no data for the Kinai, Tōkaidō, or Tōsandō for the period 820–930, almost all areas of Japan lost population, except the Hokurikudō. Losses were particularly marked for western Honshu, especially the San'indō. Second, for the era 930–1150, western Honshu continued to become depopulated, although at a lower rate than earlier. On the other hand, the Kinai and Kyushu gained modestly, and eastern Honshu expanded by anywhere from 25–33 percent.

It is difficult to assess the reasons for these trends. Between 820 and 1150, the climate may have been warmer than previous ages, perhaps prompting drought in western Japan while lengthening the growing season in northern and eastern Honshu. Moreover, western Honshu was closer to the continent, a gateway to lethal microbes that may have killed more there. In any case, we might certainly argue that the relative decline of western Japan reduced the tax base of the court more severely, while the growth of eastern Honshu may have been just one more factor in the growing power of the military families of that area.

Returning to the island-wide estimates computed by the two methods, I would suggest that they reveal two points. First, they run the gamut from somewhat lower than the 5.8–6.4 range inferred for the early eighth century to about the same. In my view, the era 715–39 could well be the peak of what Kitō defined as Japan's second demographic cycle. Second, the range 5.5–6.3 million for 1150 is significantly higher than the 4.4–5.6 number adduced for 950. It seems that there may have been some small gain in population, agriculture, or perhaps the overall economy, after all. Why did an expansion, if any, take place?

NOTES

1. Sawada Goichi, *Nara chō jidai minsei keizai no sūteki kenkyū* (Kashiwa shobō, 1972), 305–9.

2. Takahashi Bonsen, *Nihon jinkō shi no kenkyū* (San'yū sha, 1941), 1:66.

3. Kitō Hiroshi, *Nihon nisen nen no jinkō shi* (PHP Paperbacks, 1983), 45–46.

4. Dana Morris, "Land and Society," in Donald Shively and William McCullough, eds., *The Cambridge History of Japan* (Cambridge: Cambridge University Press, 1999), 2:219.

5. Kamata Motokazu, "Nihon kodai no jinkō ni tsuite," *Mokkan kenkyū* 6 (1984): 141–44.

6. SZKT, *Shoku Nihongi*, Tenpyō 19/5/1, 192.

7. Kamata, "Nihon kodai no jinkō," 142–43. The basis for Kamata's conclusion may be found in *Nihon koten bungaku taikei*, *Nihon shoki*, II, Jitō 3/Int. 8/10, 499; *Nihongi: Chronicles of Japan from the Earliest Times to A.D. 697*, translated by William Aston (London: Kegan, Trench, and Trubner, 1896), 2:394; and SZKT, *Shoku Nihongi*, Tenpyō 4/8/22, 129.

8. Kitō Hiroshi, "'Chōsa' Meiji izen Nihon no chiiki jinkō," *Jōchi keizai ronshū* 41 (March 1996): 67, 74–75. Also see his *Jinkō kara yomu Nihon no rekishi* (Kōdan sha, 2000).

9. Takeuchi Rizō, "Shōsōin koseki chōsa gaihō," *Shigaku zasshi* 68 (March 1959): 44–45. Kishi Toshio investigated the Hanyū register. Also note Imazu Katsunori, "Taihō ninen Mino no kuni Kamo no kohori Hanyū no sato koseki o megutte," *Okayama daigaku gakunai kyōdō kenkyū 'shizen to ningen no kyōsei' hōkukusho: Bungaku bu sabutema: 'Kankyō' to bunka bunmei rekishi* (Okayama: Okayama daigaku, 2003), 23–33.

10. Sawada, *Nara chō jidai*, 303. Also we may wonder why Kamata gave no consideration to mortality factors such as disease or famine and never discussed how

his estimate might apply to fertility. For a recent study raising these very factors and arguing for population stasis during the Nara and Heian periods, see Sakaue Yasutoshi, "Nara Heian jidai jinkō deeta no sai kentō," *Nihon shi kenkyū* 536 (April 2007): 1–18.

11. Sawada, *Nara chō jidai*, 298–301.

12. *Rissho zanpen 27 Kaitei shiseki shūran* (Shiseki shūran kenkyū kai, 1969), 108. Articles evaluating the historical value of this source include Sakamoto Tarō, *Sakamoto Tarō chosaku shū 7 Ritsuryō seido* (Yoshikawa kōbunkan, 1989), 155–72; Yokoyama Sadahiro, "*Rissho zanpen* ni tsuite," *Kokushi kan daigaku kyōyō ronshū* 8 (March 1979): 1–20; and Tōno Haruyuki, "*Ko rissho zanpen* shikun," *Nanto bukkyō* 46 (1981): 83–102.

13. The basis for these estimates of Japan's urban population at this time may be found in Chapter 3, Notes 78–83.

14. The classic example of this thinking is Kozo Yamamura, "The Decline of the *Ritsuryo* System: Hypotheses on Economic and Institutional Change," *Journal of Japanese Studies* 1 (autumn 1974): 1–37; and Morris, "Land and Society," 224–35.

It is interesting to observe that this explanation relies upon a public-private dichotomy shared by Japanese historians since prewar days. The only difference between Yamamura and Japanese scholars such as Torao Toshiya ("Nara Economic and Social Institutions," in Delmer M. Brown, ed., *The Cambridge History of Japan* [Cambridge: Cambridge University Press, 1993], 1:415–52), is that the former saw private interests as "good" and public ones as "bad" while Torao and his generation, possibly influenced by Confucian values, reversed the attribution. See also Chapter 2, Note 71.

15. Kitō, *Nihon nisen nen no jinkō shi*, 46–57. On this source, see *Shohon shūsei Wamyō ruijū shō: Honbun hen* (Kyoto: Rinsen shoten, 1968), 602–11, on the area of fields by province; 612–64, on the number of administrative villages (*gō*) and districts (*gun*). Also note Ikebe Wataru, ed., *Wamyō ruijū shō gun gō ri eki mei kōshō*. As is noted below, the actual area of fields contained in *Wamyō shō* tabulates to about 862,806, and this is the figure that I used later; see Iyanaga Teizō, *Nihon kodai shakai keizai shi kenkyū* (Iwanami shoten, 1980), 380–83.

16. Kitō, *Nihon nisen no jinkō shi*, 46–47. Actually, the figure comes out to 6,485,000 when we follow Kitō's original method precisely, but apparently he modified some of the provincial land totals slightly to arrive at his 6,437,600 number. The same also seems to hold true for Kitō's calculation made in 2000.

17. See Kitō, *Jinkō kara yomu Nihon no rekishi*, 56–57, where he hints at adjustments in several provincial field totals but does not go into detail. The only alteration he states for the record is a lowering of the estimate for Heian from 250,000 to 120,000.

18. Toda Yoshimi, *Nihon ryōshu sei seiritsu shi no kenkyū* (Iwanami shoten, 1967), 168–90; "Jū-jūsan seiki no nōgyō rōdō to sonraku—aratauchi o chūshin toshite," in *Chūsei shakai no seiritsu to tenkai* (Yoshikawa kōbunkan, 1976), 309–31. Readers should note that Dana Morris ("Land and Society," 183–94) has a more optimistic view of agricultural conditions.

19. Amino Yoshihiko is well known for this view. To cite two examples, see his *Nihon chūsei no hinōgyōmin to tennō* (Iwanami shoten, 1984) and *Nihon chūsei no minshū zō* (Iwanami shoten, 1980), 63–75. In 2001 Amino reasserted his thesis in *Chūsei minshū no seigyō to gijutsu* (Tokyo daigaku shuppan kai, 2001), 1.

20. William McCullough, "The Capital and Its Society," in Shively and

McCullough eds., *The Cambridge History of Japan*, 2:121–23.

21. Amino, "Chūsei no futan taikei—nengu ni tsuite," in Nagahara Keiji et al., eds., *Chūsei kinsei no kokka to shakai* (Tokyo daigaku shuppan kai, 1986), 82–86. Amino also related the same idea to me in conversation, September 1999.

22. In this regard, it is interesting to note that Minamoto Shitagō followed his tally of rice fields with a listing of each province's official amount of loan rice. Further, see Kitō's statement (in Kitō, *Jinkō kara yomu Nihon no rekishi*, 57) that his figure records only the population *that could have been sustained* by rice paddies.

23. See Takigawa Masajirō, 108–15; Sawada, *Nara chō jidai*, 463–69.

24. I arrived at the average .217 *chō* as follows. Takigawa's opinion that an allotment could support only 60 percent of a grantee's needs means that it would have taken .267 *chō* to sustain the average peasant. For Sawada, I averaged his estimate of 67–75 percent at 71 percent yielding .225 *chō*. To these two figures I added Kitō's .16 *chō*, divided by 3, and calculated .217.

25. Philip C. Brown, *Central Authority and Local Autonomy in the Formation of Early Modern Japan* (Stanford: Stanford University Press, 1993), 58–88; "The Mismeasure of Land: Land Surveying in the Tokugawa Period," *Monumenta Nipponica* 42 (summer 1987): 115–55.

26. Sakamoto Shōzō, *Nihon ōchō kokka taisei ron* (Tōkyō daigaku shuppan kai, 1972), 138–64; *Nihon no rekishi 6 Sekkan jidai* (Shōgakkan, 1974), 126–44. On the *shi shōzu*, see Kishi Toshio, *Nihon kodai sekichō no kenkyū* (Hanawa shobō, 1973), 391–414.

27. For example, see Torao, "Nara Economic and Social Institutions," 451–52. In Japanese, see Maruyama Yoshihiko, *Kodai Tōdaiji shōen no kenkyū* (Keisui sha, 2001); Ōhashi Shin'ya, "Biwa ko ni ikiru," in Hashimoto Yoshimasa, ed., *Kankyō rekishigaku no shiza* (Iwata shoin, 2002), 62–69, on the inundation of Tōdaiji's Ōmi estates by a rise in the level of Lake Biwa in the late Heian period.

28. The 20–30 percent figure is a conservative estimate from Yamamoto Takashi, (*Shōen sei no tenkai to chiiki shakai* [Tosui shobō, 1995], 104–18), who was working with Kamakura documents. Given the data cited in Note 18 above, however, this percentage, or perhaps even a higher one, seems equally applicable to the middle and late Heian era. Toda, *Nihon ryōshu sei*, 55–58, 180–82, 330–31, lists 30–50 percent. Toda's classic study of Eizanji's lands in Yamato from 990 to 1059 showed that of 35 one-*chō* units, 17 fluctuated dramatically in regard to the percentage under cultivation, while only 4 parcels were constantly and completely farmed; cf. Toda, "Chūsei no hōken ryōshu sei," in *Iwanami kōza Nihon rekishi 6 Chūsei 2* (Iwanami shoten, 1962), 231–32. Also note Harashima Reiji ("Hasseiki no inasaku ni kansuru ni san no mondai," *Rekishi hyōron* 148 [December 1962]: 24–32), who gives estimates of between 12 and 44 percent for the late eighth century. Finally, note a book review by Hayakawa Shōhachi ("Hihyō to shokai," *Shigaku zasshi* 71 [August 1962]: 97), in which he argues that the field lists contained in *Wamyō shō* included abandoned lands *(fukanden den)*. To be absolutely clear, these various cases were not mere legalities, but the surveyors recorded that there were no cultivators living there.

29. Tsude Hiroshi, *Nihon nōkō shakai no seiritsu katei* (Iwanami shoten, 1989), 67; Uno Takao, *Shōen no kōkogaku* (Aoki shoten, 2001), 61–68.

30. My estimate for Heian derives from McCullough, "The Capital and Its Society," 2:119–23. For other urban estimates, see Chapter 3, Note 78.

31. Hayami Akira, "The Population at the Beginning of the Tokugawa Period: An Introduction to the Historical Demography of Pre-Industrial Japan," *Keio Economic*

Studies 4 (1966): 22.

32. *Nōrin gyō: chōki keizai tōkei* (Tōyō keizai shinpō sha, 1966), 9:75–90.

33. Amino (*Chūsei minshū no seigyō to gijutsu*, 1) gives implicit support to this multiplier for the ancient era.

34. Kitō, *Jinkō kara yomu Nihon no rekishi*, 58. For the original source, see *Kojitsu sōsho* 22 *Shūgai shō*, 409–18. The original is sometimes difficult to read, and so I followed Iyanaga, *Kodai shakai keizai shi*, 380–83. My total of 956,558 *chō* derives from Iyanaga, who had access to several variant texts.

Readers will notice that each method leads to a somewhat different total population for Japan. This is due to the differing assumptions and data employed with each method. Because no one at this stage can say that one method is "right" and another "wrong," I used a broad range of 4.4–5.6 million to take into account all reasonable possibilities.

35. Iyanaga, *Kodai shakai keizai shi*, 363–67.

36. Kitō, *Nihon nisen nen no jinkō shi*, 12–13, 47.

37. Kitō, *Jinkō kara yomu Nihon no rekishi*, 16–17, 58.

38. Amino, "Chūsei no futan taikei—nengu ni tsuite," 82–86.

39. Satō Yasuhiro, "Heian jidai no kuni no kendan," *Shirin* 75 (September 1991): 33–68; Satō Yasuhiro, *Nihon chūsei no rinmei* (Kyōtō daigaku gakujutsu shuppan kai, 2001), 49–97.

40. Toda Yoshimi, "Jū-jūsan seiki no nōgyō rōdō to sonraku—aratauchi o chūshin toshite," in *Chūsei shakai no seiritsu to tenkai* (Yoshikawa kōbunkan, 1976), 309–31; "Chūsei no hōken ryōshu sei," 231–32. The 20–30 percent figure is a conservative estimate taken from Yamamoto Takashi, *Shōen sei no tenkai* (Tosui shobō, 1995), 104–18. Given the data cited in Toda (see Note 28), however, this percentage, or perhaps even a higher one, seems equally applicable to the middle and late Heian era; see Toda, *Nihon ryōshu sei*, 55–58, 180–82, 330–31.

41. Ishii Susumu, *Kamakura bushi no jitsuzō* (Heibon sha, 1987), 109.

42. For comparison's sake, Hayami Akira argues that even in the late Edo period about 1 *tan* of paddy field was required to sustain a person per year; see Hayami Akira and Miyamoto Matao, "Gaisetsu: jūnana juhasseiki," in their *Nihon keizai shi* 1 *Keizai shakai no seiritsu jūnana jūhasseiki* (Iwanami shoten 1988), 44. It should be noted that the figures in the table for 1600, 1650, and 1700 are all Hayami's estimates, and therefore lead to the seemingly high *tan* per person figures. If Hayami's estimates for overall population are too low, as many believe, then the average *tan* per person would fall.

Moreover, Hayami's number is merely an average from the more productive farmland in Japan; a record from southern Kyushu in the 1600s showed 4 and even 6 *tan* necessary to support one villager; see *Kinsei Iriki monjo*, edited by Abe Yoshio et al. (Tōkyō daigaku shuppan kai, 1981), 433–51. We should further note that the twelfth-century *tan* was about 30 percent larger than the Edo measure, making Kitō's figure even larger relative to that needed to sustain a person in the Tokugawa period.

For the record, if the yield from 1 average-grade *tan* was 1.57 *koku*, as per Sawada, 466, and it required 2.17 *koku* to sustain an individual in 750 (or even 950), then a total of 3.4069 *koku* would have been necessary for a year (1.57 X 2.17 = 3.4069). If the annual requirement for a person's sustenance remained unchanged in 1150, but the same volume (3.4069 *koku*) could be harvested from only 1.975 *tan*, then the yield from 1 *tan* in 1150 would have come to about 1.73 *koku*, an improvement of .16 *koku* (or .04 *koku* per *tan* per year). This hypothetical figure is well in line with the discussion of agriculture below. Of course, given the numerous unknowns, there is no need to suppose that the 1.975 *tan* is the only reasonable estimate. In general, higher divisors lead to a smaller overall population with lower yields; lower divisors have the opposite effect.

43. No one knows the number of urban residents in Japan in 1150. For my tabulations, see Chapter 3, notes 78–83. Since it has been estimated that Japan's urbanites in 1590 numbered about 5 percent of the population, it is highly unlikely that the number exceeded 200,000 in 1150; see Kitō Hiroshi, *Edo jidai no jinkō* (Jōchi daigaku, 1990), 77–78.

44. Readers will again note that, as with the estimates for 950, the two totals for 1150 differ, one being 5.5–6.1 million and the other 5.9–6.3 million. As in the earlier case, the minute difference derives from the differing assumptions applied in each method. Rather than provide one number (about 6.8 million) as Kitō did, I felt it was more prudent to give a range of 5.5–6.3 million because no one can prove that one method will produce a more credible result than the other. In any case, I think that Kitō's figure is too high and fails to take into consideration many of the points I have raised.

Table 4. Population (A), Administrative Villages (B), and Arable Land (C)
by Province in Japan, 820–927, according to Sawada

Province	Pop (A)	Admin Vil (B)	A/B	Arable Land (C)	C/B
Kinai					
Yamshiro (1)	99,600	78	1,277	8,961	115
Yamshiro (2)	49,800	same	640	same	same
Yamato (1)	130,300	89	1,464	17,905	201
Yamato (2)	65,200	same	730	same	same
Kawachi (1)	94,200	80	1,178	11,338	142
Kawachi (2)	65,200	same	590	same	same
Izumi (1)	53,500	24	2,229	4,569	190
Izumi (2)	26,700	same	1,110	same	same
Settsu (1)	112,000	78	1,446	12,525	161
Settsu (2)	56,400	same	720	same	same
Tōkaidō					
Iga	37,300	18	2,072	4,051	225
Ise	108,800	94	1,157	18,130	193
Owari	55,400	69	803	6,820	99
Mikawa	56,000	69	812	6,820	99
Tōtōmi	90,800	96	946	13,611	142
Suruga	75,500	59	1,280	9,063	154
Kai	68,700	31	2,216	12,249	395
Izu	21,000	21	1,000	2,110	100
Sagami	102,000	67	1,522	11,236	168
Musashi	130,900	119	1,100	35,574	299
Awa	40,200	32	1,256	4,335	135
Kazusa	125,800	76	1,655	22,846	301
Shimōsa	120,600	91	1,325	26,432	290
Hitachi	216,900	153	1,418	40,092	262
Tōsandō					
Ōmi	141,900	93	1,526	33,402	359
Mino	115,150	131	879	14,823	113
Hida	13,850	13	1,065	6,615	509
Shinano	101,750	67	1,519	30,908	461
Kōzuke	134,600	102	1,320	30,937	303
Shimotsuke	99,850	70	1,426	30,155	431
Mutsu	186,000	188	989	51,440	274
Dewa	80,300	71	1,131	26,109	368
Hokurikudō					
Sado	19,500	22	886	3,960	180

Province	Pop (A)	Admin Vil (B)	A/B	Arable Land (C)	C/B
Wakasa	28,600	21	1,362	3,077	147
Echizen	120,800	55	2,196	12,066	219
Kaga	80,600	30	2,687	13,767	459
Noto	53,750	26	2,076	8,205	316
Etchū	82,300	42	1,960	17,909	426
Echigo	97,350	34	2,863	14,997	441
San'indō					
Tanba	87,400	68	1,285	10,666	157
Tango	49,950	35	1,427	4,756	136
Tajima	95,600	59	1,620	7,555	128
Inaba	94,600	50	1,892	7,914	158
Hōki	77,600	48	1,617	8,161	170
Izumo	82,100	78	1,053	9,435	121
Iwami	47,550	37	1,285	4,884	132
Oki	8,800	12	733	585	49
San'yōdō					
Harima	145,650	98	1,486	21,414	219
Mimasaka	98,450	64	1,538	11,021	172
Bizen	114,350	51	2,242	13,185	259
Bitchū	89,950	72	1,249	10,227	142
Bingo	72,900	65	1,122	9,301	143
Aki	65,600	63	1,041	7,357	117
Suō	58,950	45	1,310	7,834	174
Nagato	40,750	40	1,019	4,603	115
Nankaidō					
Kii	55,150	56	985	7,198	129
Awaji	13,600	17	800	2,650	156
Awa	66,950	46	1,455	3,414	74
Sanuki	106,200	90	1,180	18,647	207
Iyo	101,100	72	1,404	13,501	188
Tosa	60,700	43	1,412	6,451	150
Saikaidō					
Chikuzen	89,150	102	874	18,500	181
Chikugo	74,300	54	1,376	12,800	237
Buzen	73,450	43	1,708	13,200	307
Bungo	84,950	47	1,807	7,500	160
Hizen	83,400	44	1,895	13,900	316
Higo	181,750	99	1,836	23,500	237
Hyūga	45,750	28	1,634	4,800	171
Ōsumi	24,750	37	669	4,800	130

Province	Pop (A)	Admin Vil (B)	A/B	Arable Land (C)	C/B
Satsuma	22,950	35	658	4,800	137
Iki	10,000	11	909	620	56

Source: Sawada Goichi, *Nara chō jidai minsei keizai no sūteki kenkyū*, 298–300. Arable land is given in *chō*. Column A contains Sawada's population estimate for the named province. Column B lists the number of administrative villages, which by law were supposed to have about fifty households. Column A/B computes the number of persons per administrative village. Column C notes the arable land in the named province, and Column C/B calculates the arable per administrative village.

Sawada provided two estimates for each province in the Kinai because he felt that Mutsu's ratio of taxable adults to total population may have been inapplicable for the capital region. The figures for Kaga should be included with those for Echizen. Ōsumi estimates include averages for Tanegashima.

Table 5. Population by Province, Early Ninth, Tenth, and Mid-Twelfth Centuries

Province	829	927	935	1150
Yamashiro	-----	99,600/49,800	50,303	55,263
Yamato	-----	130,300/65,200	100,505	104,878
Kawachi	-----	88,100/47,100	63,639	67,696
Izumi	-----	53,500/26,700	25,651	25,445
Settsu	-----	112,800/56,400	70,302	69,774
Kinai Total	-----	484,300/245,200	310,400	323,056
Iga	-----	37,300	25,320	25,008
Ise	-----	108,800	101,768	117,333
Shima	-----	6,500	696	30,324
Owari	-----	55,400	38,286	73,573
Mikawa	-----	56,000	38,286	43,503
Tōtōmi	-----	90,800	76,397	79,969
Suruga	-----	75,500	50,870	60,419
Izu	-----	21,000	11,843	17,354
Kai	-----	68,700	68,758	61,936
Sagami	-----	102,000	63,067	70,835

Province	829	927	935	1150
Musahi	-----	130,900	199,679	317,852
Awa	-----	40,200	24,338	26,901
Kazusa	-----	125,800	128,238	139,783
Shimōsa	-----	120,600	148,366	203,513
Hitachi	232,000	216,900	225,038	259,252
Tokaidō Total	-----	1,256,400	1,200,950	1,527,555
Ōmi	-----	141,900	187,488	206,289
Mino	126,900	103,400	83,200	279,394
Hida	15,200	12,500	37,135	26,864
Shinano	98,400	105,100	173,489	188,220
Kōzuke	165,000	104,200	173,646	175,472
Shimotsuke	97,000	102,700	169,263	169,348
Mutsu	186,000	186,000	288,728	277,994
Dewa	58,000	102,600	146,547	238,228
Tosandō Total	746,500	858,400	1,259,496	1,561,809
Wakasa	28,900	28,300	20,863	19,358
Echizen	158,400	120,800	67,725	145,395
Kaga	-----	80,600	77,273	77,311
Noto	62,200	45,300	46,059	52,291
Etchū	65,900	98,700	100,527	131,970
Echigo	96,800	97,900	84,182	146,394
Sado	18,800	20,200	22,227	30,034
Hokurikudō Total	431,000	491,800	418,856	602,753
Tanba	96,800	78,000	59,867	66,944
Tango	49,200	50,700	26,695	34,147
Tajima	104,200	87,000	42,411	47,752
Inaba	105,600	83,600	44,426	49,435
Hōki	78,200	77,000	45,812	54,529
Izumo	82,500	81,700	52,963	61,474
Iwami	49,200	45,900	27,419	30,046
Oki	9,400	8,200	3,284	3,848
San'indō Total	575,100	512,100	302,877	348,175
Harima	144,700	146,600	120,195	130,964
Mimasaka	107,100	89,800	61,860	71,637
Bizen	116,300	112,400	74,012	81,443
Bitchū	92,600	87,300	57,409	67,116
Bingo	72,400	73,400	52,206	57,342
Province	829	927	935	1150

Province	829	927	935	1150
Aki	59,300	71,900	41,300	46,154
Suō	52,100	65,800	43,971	47,221
Nagato	39,100	42,400	25,836	29,411
San'yōdō Total	683,600	689,600	476,789	531,288
Kii	55,000	55,300	40,407	43,904
Awaji	12,300	14,900	14,874	17,700
Awa	74,400	59,500	19,168	32,346
Sanuki	108,500	103,900	104,669	110,656
Iyo	107,100	95,100	75,780	91,427
Tosa	59,300	62,100	36,209	38,069
Nankaidō Total	416,600	390,800	291,107	334,102
Chikuzen	85,400	92,900	103,839	121,893
Chikugo	75,300	73,300	71,845	70,163
Buzen	75,300	71,600	74,090	81,535
Bungo	82,500	87,400	42,097	46,685
Hizen	85,400	81,400	78,019	83,021
Higo	178,000	185,500	131,903	144,692
Hyūga	47,700	43,800	26,942	51,175
Ōsumi	17,400	18,400	26,942	29,028
Satsuma	17,400	28,500	26,942	34,048
Iki	9,400	10,600	3,480	3,824
Tsushima	-----	7,000	2,402	3,824
Tanegashima	-----	3,700	(no data)	(no data)
Saikaidō Total	673,800	714,100	588,501	669,888
Grand Total	3,758,600	5,397,500	4,848,976	5,898,626
		5,144,275		

Source: Sawada Goichi, *Nara chō jidai minsei keizai no sūteki kenkyū*, 187–91, 261, 270–76. Sawada computed estimates for 820 and 927 by means of the loan rice method. It should be noted that he supplied two estimates for the five provinces of the Kinai, and thus two grand totals are indicated for his work. The figures listed for 935 were tabulated from rice field totals in *Wamyō shō* as listed in the chart in Iyanaga, *Nihon kodai shakai keizai shi*, 380–83, according to the second method devised in this chapter. The lone figure for Hitachi Province in 820 follows Kamata, "Nihon kodai no jinkō ni tsuite," 141. The numbers for 1150 were calculated from rice totals in *Shūgai shō*, as listed in the chart in Iyanaga, *Nihon Kodai shakai keizai shi*, 380–83, according to the second method described in this article. Note that many provinces have no data in *The Ordinances of Kōnin* (820).

Table 6. Regional Demographic Variations, 820–1150*

Region	820–930	930–1150
Kinai	-------	4%
Tōkaidō	-------	27
Tōsandō	-------	24
Hokurikudō	5.30%	35.20%
San'indō	-41%	-14.50%
San'yōdō	-10%	-8.30%
Nankaidō	-18.20%	-2%
Saikaidō	-3.30%	2.90%

*I computed the population for each region for 930 by averaging the two figures for 927 and 935.

CHAPTER 2
Mortality Variables

Given no significant in- or out-migration, a population total is the product of fluctuating birth and death rates, which are in turn influenced by a long list of factors drawn from myriad aspects of the human experience. In terms of mortality, pestilence, famine, and war are the phenomena most frequently cited. To put my estimates to a rigorous test, I shall examine extraordinary causes of death and then turn to indirect variables affecting fertility and longevity or otherwise defining demographic trends, such as land clearance and agricultural technology; settlement patterns and migration; the labor market and industry; trade/urbanization; family, marriage, and kinship patterns; and the level of popular material well-being. To be authoritative, a discussion should not omit the inconvenient but account for all components, integrating as many as possible into an overarching interpretation.

DISEASE

This section will present pertinent new data along with two fresh approaches to the subject of pestilence. First, it will offer further evidence of heavy mortality during the eighth, ninth, and tenth centuries, suggesting that the smallpox epidemic of 735–37 (described previously in *Population, Disease, and Land*) was not unusual. Second, it will explore archaeological and magico-religious documentation; this was unnoted in *Population, Disease, and Land* but has grown in volume and importance over the last twenty years. Finally, the section will conclude with a general observation about pestilence and the decline of the Chinese-style (*ritsuryō;* 645–900) and dynastic, or classical (*ōchō;* 900–1100), states.

At the risk of belaboring the obvious, I should note that, according to William McNeill's hypothesis, the archipelago had relatively little experience with killer infections because of their geographic isolation from the Asian mainland and from each other until the late seventh century, when the court established Chinese-style systems of taxation and transit. As of the late 600s, therefore, the islands were home to a dense population with little or no immunity to infectious diseases. Also, beginning around 700, killer viruses and bacteria entered and were more easily able to move about this fertile breeding ground, resulting in widespread epidemics with heavy mortality every generation. The critical biological factor in this proposition was that immunities gained by survivors of an infection in one generation could not be passed along to offspring, who then awaited another visitation—which usually occurred during their adulthood—to determine their fate. In McNeill's view, this pattern of repeated die-off and recovery, with the resultant demographic stasis or even decline, continued until after 1200.

Fortunately, in the thirty years since the publication of *Plagues and Peoples*, Japanese historians have evinced a growing interest in environmental history and natural disasters, including pestilential ravages. Regarding the relatively well-known eighth century, one scholar has concentrated his energies on the smallpox epidemic of 735–37, tabulating the percentage of aristocrats holding the Fifth Court Rank and above who died during the outbreak. He has shown that 36 of 92, or 39.1percent, of highly placed nobles noted in the *Shoku Nihongi* succumbed to the illness. Furthermore, he has argued that the court enacted at least thirteen new policies—everything from a ban on nongovernmental rice loans to an alteration in the Chinese characters for Yamato province—in the wake of the disaster. Overall, this younger scholar estimates that 40–50 percent of the archipelago's inhabitants died during this particular attack of the smallpox virus.[1]

One weakness in McNeill's thesis is the lack of similarly precise death tolls for the scantily documented early and middle Heian eras. Thanks to the work of Fujikawa Yū and Hattori Toshirō, we can now remedy this dearth of statistics to some degree.[2] The first example originates from the poorly documented late ninth century. In an entry for 870, *Nihon sandai jitsuroku*, the last of the court's *Six National Histories (Rikkoku shi)*, records that during 865 and 866 an unknown infection killed 3,189 residents of Oki Province.[3] Fortunately, Sawada Goichi made an estimate of Oki's early ninth-century population: 9,400. Thus mortality from this two-year pestilence was 33.9 percent if we credit Sawada's calculation as being accurate. Moreover, in another Sawada tabulation done for the early tenth century, Oki's population shows a decline to only 8,200 persons, a fact attributable to plagues such as the one that struck in 865–66.

To be sure, Oki is an island, and would have been subject to the same "island epidemiology" from which Hawai'i and Japan itself suffered. There is at least one more good case with mortality statistics, however, to suggest that Oki's ninth-century experience with microparasites was anything but exceptional. In his classic work, Fujikawa cites two reliable court histories, *Nihon kiryaku* and *Hyakuren shō*, to describe a foreign-borne pestilential outbreak, quite probably smallpox, occurring during 993–95.[4] In the entry, annalists tell us that more than 60 persons of the Fifth Court Rank and above died in 994 alone; a note for the next year places this number more precisely at 69.

Although historians have no way of knowing the exact number of nobles holding the Fifth Rank or higher in the late tenth century, it is possible to infer a number from eighth-century statistics.[5] During the first half of the 700s, sources suggest that there were on average about 135 persons in this category. Of course, over the late eighth, ninth, and tenth centuries this elite group expanded considerably, although central government retrenchment made the status less remunerative after 800. Assuming that aristocrats holding the Fifth Rank and higher numbered 300 in 994, a figure considerably higher than at any time in the 700s, we would obtain a mortality of 23.3 percent. If the figure was 350, then the death toll falls to about 20 percent.

In either case, application of this mortality to all Heian, a city of about 100,000, leads to catastrophic results. Furthermore, it seems safe to assume that dwellers in an urban center with a long history of contact with various infections would have had greater immunity and lower mortality than most peasants in the less-densely settled countryside, where smallpox also raged. As an aside, political historians like to note that this era corresponded to the time when Fujiwara no Michinaga began his ascent to power—thanks to a generous assist from the deaths of his rivals in this plague.[6]

To those familiar with the limitations of primary source material for the ninth and tenth centuries, these two cases would seem to bolster McNeill's thesis considerably. Other examples, drawn from the provinces but lacking precise statistics, enhance McNeill's case even further. For instance, from Tōji's Ōyama-no-shō in Tanba Province in 1009: "Recently, many people have vanished, and there are no cultivators. For this reason land has gone out of cultivation for a long time."[7] We can only infer a plague from the Ōyama case, but for Daigoji's 60-chō Sone-no-shō in Ise in 1017, the record states: "The amount of land currently under cultivation in this estate is even less than 20 chō. This is because of frequent epidemics; estate officials and cultivators have mostly died."[8] Or again for Iwashimizu Hachimangū's Izumie-no-shō in Mino for 1023: "But last year during the great epidemic, estate officials and the cultivators all died. Most land went out of cultivation."[9] Or for Tōdaiji's Kuroda-no-shō in Iga in 1041: "But the long-time residents of this district have died or fled. Thereafter, there has not been even one resident for several decades."[10] These examples cluster around central Honshu, but mortality may have been even more severe in peripheral regions where more infrequent contact with a killer infection led to lesser immunity and a higher number of susceptibles.

A Tale of Flowering Fortunes, the fictionalized account of Fujiwara rule, also reveals how lethal epidemic outbreaks could be in the middle Heian period. For 974, the author wrote: "A smallpox epidemic raged among all classes of the populace, striking terror into every heart and killing gently born men and women in appalling numbers."[11] This same tale describes the "terrible" pestilence of 995 noted above. During 1019–22, *A Tale* gives its readers a textbook example of how foreign-borne plagues wreaked havoc and death: "According to reports from Tsukushi [northern Kyushu], everyone in that region had been sick since the preceding year. Because more than two decades had elapsed since the [prior] epidemic, most people had acquired no immunity to the disease, and there was great alarm and agitation at Court and elsewhere."[12] Eventually, the smallpox virus reached the capital, causing many high-born to die in a great uproar. *A Tale* also records epidemic outbreaks for 998, 1000, and 1025, and usually the depictions show the pathogen as entering from Kyushu, a certain indication of its overseas origin. The entries also state that most residents of the archipelago had no immunities because the previous outbreak had occurred before they were born. Over the epoch from 698 until 1061, a smallpox epidemic swept the islands an average of every thirty years.

Even as late as the first fifty years of the twelfth century, indications are that pestilence was still ravaging a vulnerable populace. Altogether, sixteen years witnessed epidemics, not quite the incidence of the horrific eighth or ninth centuries but still enough to make infections a leading cause of death. Significantly, smallpox, the grisly killer that had visited the islands about every generation since its introduction in the sixth century, came only three times: in 1113, 1125–26, and 1143. While this rate was more frequent than formerly, the outbreaks were still well spaced enough to take as their main victims young adults heading into their prime, which had a most debilitating effect on the society and its tax base. Measles is reported to have ravaged the populace twice, but since the years of its occurrence (1113 and 1127) coincide with those of smallpox epidemics, there is a strong possibility that medical authorities confused the two.

There was another less familiar but nonetheless deadly visitor: influenza. Raging in 1134–35 and 1150, each bout left an indelible imprint upon late Heian society. The outbreak of 1134–35 was particularly virulent, striking at "all under heaven" *(tenka)*.[13] As early as 1132 there had been reports of an unknown pestilence, but from the spring of 1134 the weather had turned damp and windy, conditions that played a major role in the infection's spread.[14] Because the disease afflicted everyone *(banjin)*, the year 1134 was also a bad time for agriculture, and the harvest failed in many provinces. Dense fog and rain closed down the dirt roads leading into Kyoto, and grain shortages resulted in famine the next year and on into 1136.

The court's response to the crisis also hints at the depth of the suffering. It made doles of grain, especially to the beggars and orphans wandering

Kyoto's streets. Officials also granted tax relief. As usually had been the case, the subsistence crisis brought on by the influenza epidemic led to increased social stresses, and both "evil monks" (akusō) and shrine attendants (ji'nin) used the disaster to provoke mayhem. In the Inland Sea, people who made their living with boats turned to piracy, later to be suppressed by Taira no Tadamori and his troops. Ultimately, the court resorted to debt forgiveness (tokusei) to aid needy subjects. There is no way to compute the mortality or even know the number of provinces afflicted by the epidemic, but as in the previous four centuries, disease had triggered death, famine, and social upheaval.[15]

Unfortunately, only a few of these outbreaks scattered over the Nara and Heian periods speak explicitly to the issue of death rates. More indirect but equally compelling evidence, however, has been turning up in archaeological excavations. The relevant artifacts are of four types: (1) wooden human figures (hitogata); (2) pots with human faces (jinmen bokusho doki); (3) clay horses (doba); and (4) model ovens (mokei kamado).[16] (See Figures 1–4.) According to Kaneko Hiroyuki of the Nara National Cultural Properties Research Institute, the leading expert on these relics, court priests utilized these objects in a ritsuryō ritual known as ōharae, a purification rite overseen by the aristocracy twice a year during the last day of the sixth and twelfth months. Furthermore, the government also performed ōharae at moments of crisis, such as wars, political turmoil, and natural disasters. Historical sources attest that the court enacted the ceremony in an attempt to stop an epidemic.[17] What is most important, however, is that each item has its own story tying it directly to disease.

Archaeologists excavated a wooden figure, for example, from a large ditch that served as a sewer, located east of the Imperial Palace in Nara.[18] This 11-centimeter hitogata was dated to the first half of the eighth century and bore several ink marks around an eye. On the back, someone had written: "Made due to illness of the left eye." From this and other examples, Kaneko has suggested how these wooden figures functioned. After attendants had carved a hitogata in the image of the sick individual, an exorcist cast a spell (majinai). If the spell worked, the affliction would be transferred to the figure and the patient would be cured.

Hitogata appear most frequently at sites throughout Japan's ancient capitals of the eighth century: Fujiwara, Nagaoka, and most especially Nara.[19] Archaeologists, who commonly unearth these figures in large numbers, discovered 207 hitogata at an excavation just outside Mibu Gate leading into Nara Palace.[20] Their proximity to the Palace is unsurprising since the great capitals were home to the loftiest aristocracy, the highest concentrations of susceptibles, and hence the most frequent ōharae ceremonies.

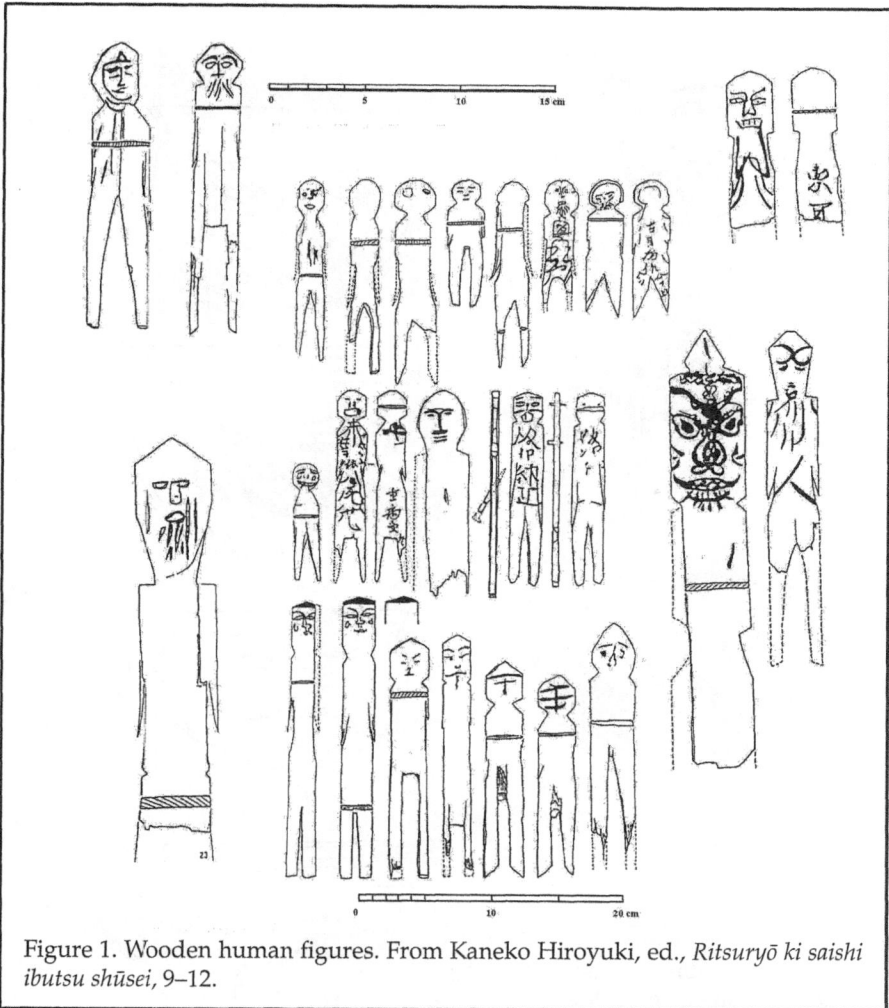

Figure 1. Wooden human figures. From Kaneko Hiroyuki, ed., *Ritsuryō ki saishi ibutsu shūsei*, 9–12.

What is surprising is that these wooden figures keep coming to light throughout the countryside: They have been found at more than forty sites as of 1988. A good example was excavated from Iba in Shizuoka, a site thought possibly to have been a district headquarters. The image bore the name Wakayamatobe Kotojime, complete with a caption suggesting illness. As in the case previously cited, this *hitogata* was undoubtedly whittled in an attempt to heal poor Kotojime.[21]

The second type of artifact, "pots with human faces in ink," has an even closer link to epidemics.[22] Archaeologists almost always uncover

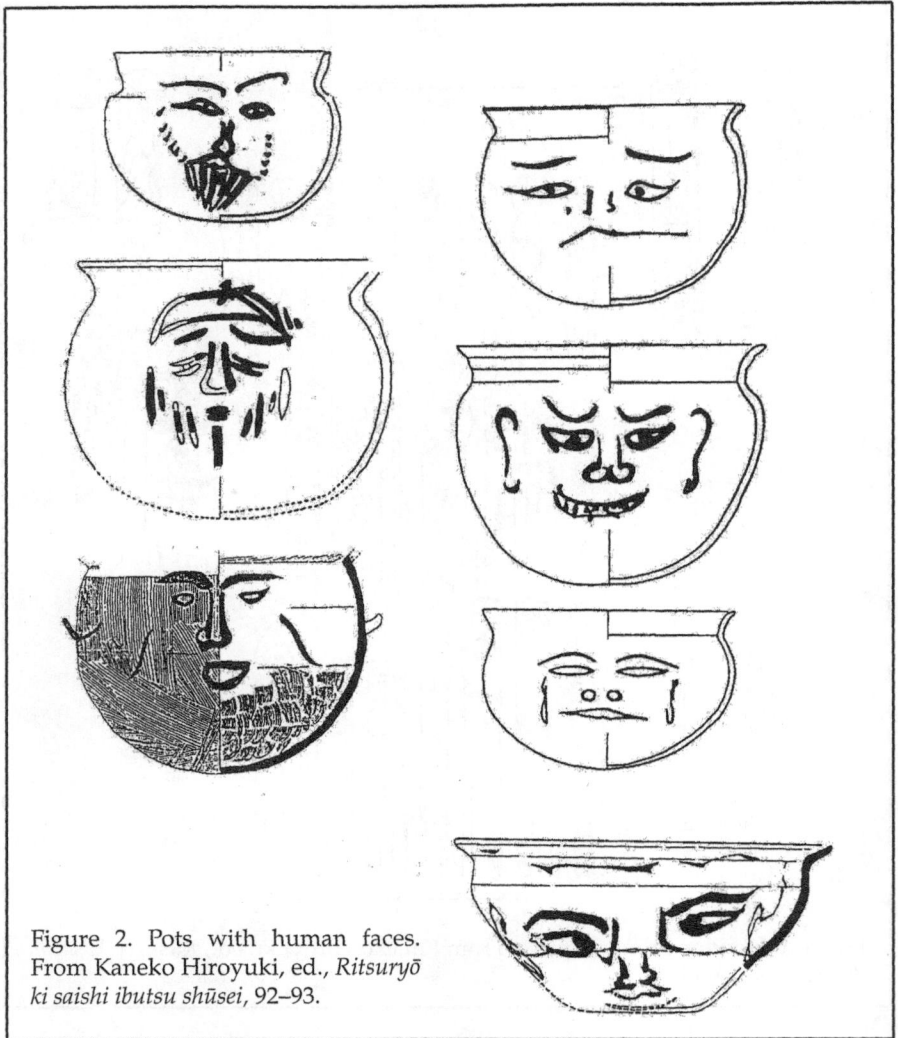

Figure 2. Pots with human faces. From Kaneko Hiroyuki, ed., *Ritsuryō ki saishi ibutsu shūsei*, 92–93.

these *jinmen doki* from the beds of streams, ditches, or sewers. According to Kaneko, relatives painted these pots (Haji ware) with the fearsome face of the epidemic god *(ekishin)*. The victim of the infection blew his or her breath into the pot, which was then covered with an earthenware or paper lid—or perhaps even left open. (A similar ritual has been recorded for the Heavenly Sovereign [*tennō*] himself in both *Engi shiki* and *Saikyūki*.)[23] During pestilence, the reasoning goes, movers collected and transported all the pots of the afflicted to a stream or sewer and dumped them, in hopes that the waters would wash away the disease spirit and the sick would recover.

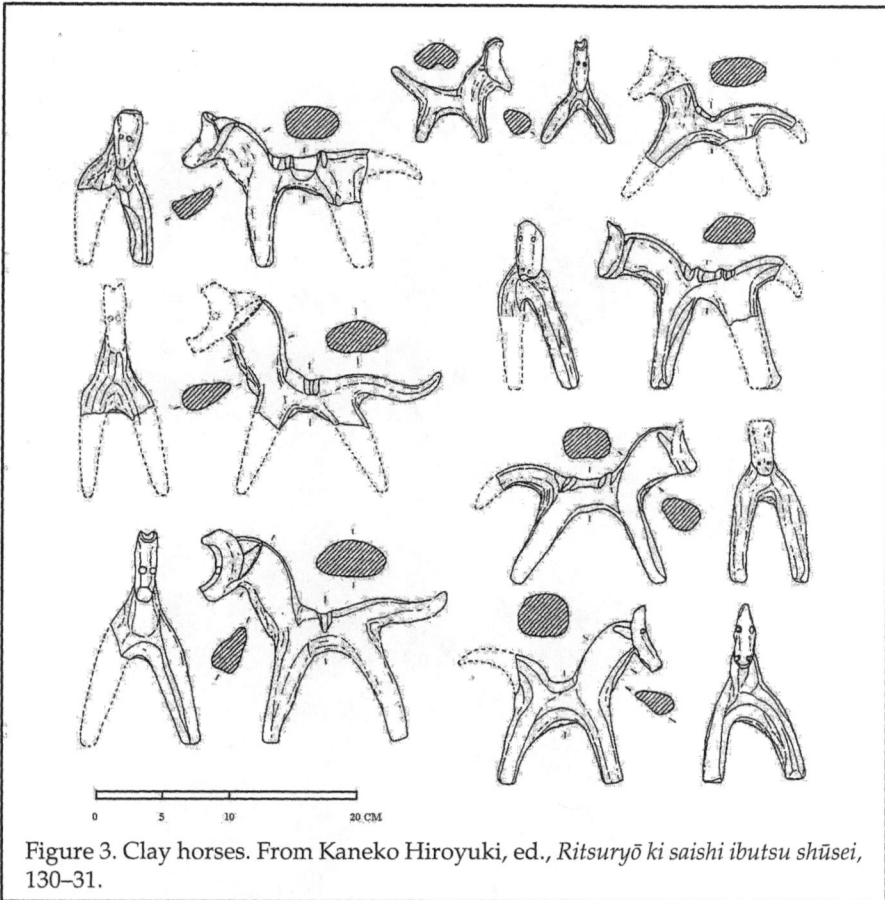

Figure 3. Clay horses. From Kaneko Hiroyuki, ed., *Ritsuryō ki saishi ibutsu shūsei*, 130–31.

The location and broken condition of many pots support such a hypothesis. Finally, a late tenth-century tale bears testimony to the curative effects of water, when it describes the pestilence-ridden populace of Heian bearing palanquins of the epidemic god to Naniwa, where the ocean would wash carriages away in the purifying waters near the "wave-bright" capital.[24]

As of 1988, the great capitals comprised the chief sites for such artifacts: 17 at Nara and 13 at Nagaoka. Many excavations contained numerous *jin-men doki*; 509 were found in a ditch excavated in a southwest corner of Nara city. Like the wooden figures, pots with human faces appear throughout the rest of Japan. By 1988 artifacts had been uncovered from twenty locations ranging from Tohoku to northern Kyushu.[25]

"Clay horses" are the third relic closely associated with epidemic outbreaks. While the usual interpretation links these artifacts to water, a

Figure 4. Model ovens.

substance itself related to *ōharae* and thus pestilence, according to the work of Mizuno Masayoshi, the horse was a symbol of disease, which could race through a settlement like an equestrian soldier.[26] Here the parallel with the European "Four Horsemen of the Apocalypse" is intriguing. Mizuno further asserts that one could put a halt to the pestilence only by breaking the legs off the miniature. Many *doba* have been recovered in just such a shattered state.[27]

Like the previous artifacts, excavators usually uncover clay horses from old ditches or streambeds. While these *doba* have come to light at more than 550 sites as of 1988, most have been found in the capital region: more than 30 percent in Nara prefecture and about 17 in Kyoto, home to both Nagaoka and Heian. In these excavations, it is not unusual to find hundreds at a time.[28]

A fourth relic, the miniature oven, also seems to have had a link to disease. The oven was a Chinese invention, which was introduced to the islands via Korea. According to Chinese beliefs, the god of the hearth protected or punished the resident family every winter, according to their just deserts, and one form of punishment was visitation by sickness. To prevent such a disaster, family members molded a small clay oven, where the god was thought to reside, and smashed the replica to chase the divinity away. These artifacts are much less common than the other three, being found at only thirteen places in Nara as of 1988.[29]

It would be a mistake to assume that every one of these artifacts can be equated with an epidemic or the ōharae ritual. If we posit that even some were related to pestilence, however, a few further points seem in order. First, the discovery of these various artifacts at centers of transportation, whether in the great capitals or in the provinces, suggests some ancient understanding of how infections were transmitted, even though preventive steps were always ceremonial. Historical sources speak of conducting purification rites "at the four corners" of the capital and the "ten boundaries of the Kinai," while legal records state that the court was not to allow "those coming from outside the capital"—undoubtedly including "impure" (in the eyes of the court) foreign embassies—into the city when ōharae ceremonies were in progress.[30]

Second, Kaneko has delimited the time period during which these four types of artifacts were most common.[31] Despite the criticisms of Izumi Takeshi, an employee at Tenri City, who argues for a Tomb-era origin for some items, Kaneko asserts that these relics usually date from the late seventh century and disappear by about 900.[32] In other words, Kaneko holds that they were ritsuryō ritual implements, associated with the court's adoption of Chinese-style institutions. Yet there is another related, and I believe more important and overlooked, point. Wooden images, pots with human faces, miniature horses, and ovens become most prominent in excavations from this period because the late seventh century is when epidemics from abroad first—insofar as records inform us—became a frequent and lethal visitor to the Japanese islands. In other words, the archaeological record supports written texts regarding the beginning of Japan's "age of microparasitism."

In addition, recently a Korean scholar has begun to mine Silla records for evidence about disease and his work bolsters the contention that the period from about 650 until 900 witnessed an East Asian pandemic.[33] He has found that smallpox and other pathogens first entered the Korean peninsula during the wars of unification during the late seventh century, having been introduced by Tang armies then allied with Silla. Furthermore, just as in the case of Japan, the population of the Korean peninsula was not dense enough to allow these various afflictions to become endemic "childhood" diseases. Thus the Silla kingdom, like Japan, suffered from repeated and severe epidemic outbreaks throughout its history. Korean records help to confirm that the onset of Japan's epidemic siege was the late seventh century, proving yet again that war and disease go hand-in-hand.

The dwindling number of *hitogata* and related artifacts in sites after about 900 does not mean that epidemics were no longer a factor in Japanese life; this will be apparent from the approach employed next. Rather, it connotes that the magico-religious terms by which people understood and tried to defend themselves against microbes had changed. While many scholars have been slow to grasp the import of plagues in social and economic terms, researchers have long recognized the important role played by disease in Heian religion. Furthermore, in the last decade or so two excellent English-language articles have emphasized the tie between pestilence and Heian combinatory magico-religious rituals: Neil McMullin on the Gion Cult in *The History of Religions* and Alan Grapard on "departed spirit" (*goryō, onryō*) rituals in the recently published Heian Japan volume of *The Cambridge History of Japan*.[34] There is a massive and nuanced literature in Japanese, but reference to the work of McMullin and Grapard will suffice to outline the basics.[35]

The belief that pestilence is a divine curse is found in almost every society, and ancient Japan was no exception. Even in the first half of the eighth century, the court frequently sent prayers to the *kami* and had pertinent sutras intoned to halt an outbreak of disease.[36] By the 770s, the court was performing rites to the "god of epidemics," often at the four corners of the capital and the ten boundaries of the Kinai and probably using the ritual artifacts described above.

After the move to the new capital at Heian in 794, rites to the epidemic god underwent a slow transformation. In 863 the historical record notes for the first time the performance of the "departed spirit" ritual (*goryō-e*).[37] As Grapard states, the basic idea behind *goryō* was that "the spirit of a departed aristocrat forced into an unjust and politically motivated death, or some cosmic power, was responsible for epidemics."[38] Perhaps Sugawara no Michizane is the most memorable example, but in 863 the court was trying to assuage the vengeful spirits of Prince Sawara (implicated in the murder of Fujiwara no Tanetsugu in the transfer to Nagaoka) and several others. From the late ninth century, rites for departed spirits became common in Heian and the countryside, given greater weight by the sad story of Michizane, the aristocrat banished in a coup by his Fujiwara enemies.

Goryō beliefs are not found in either Korea or China, and they may represent a unique Japanese notion of governmental responsibility linking misdeeds among the political elite with pestilential outbreak. In fact, according to one tradition, such a belief may have dated back to the death of Prince Nagaya, forced by the Fujiwara to commit suicide in 729.[39] One source states that after his demise, Nagaya's corpse was borne by water to Tosa, where most residents died in an epidemic.

For a while after the move to Heian, officials performed *goryō* rites at various temples and religious sites, including Tōji, Saiji, Kinugasa, and Murasakino.[40] From the late tenth century, however, Gion Shrine was the chief shrine-temple multiplex for the "departed spirit" rite. Like other such complexes, Gion had its own core mythology, which has come down to us in many variants and is neatly summarized by McMullin.[41] The chief deity was called the "Bull-Headed King of the *Devas*," or *Gozu tennō*, who set out on a journey of 80,000 *li*. Tiring along the way, he sought lodgings, first with a wealthy younger brother named Kotan Shōrai and then with a poor elder sibling named Somin Shōrai. Only Somin took in the heavenly sojourner, so he and his descendants were granted protection from disease. This could be guaranteed by displaying a sign that stated that the dwelling's inhabitants were related to Somin and invoking the Taoist magical formula "Urgently, urgently, just as in the law codes" *(Kyū kyū ritsuryō no gotoshi)*. Upon his return home, the god destroyed Kotan and anyone else not displaying the sign, while sparing Somin and his family.

As McMullin notes, it is still possible in Japan today to find homes with signs saying "This is a house of the offspring of Somin Shorai. Urgently, urgently, just as in the law codes" to ward off sickness.[42] Archaeologists have found similar wooden tablets in excavations at ancient and medieval sites, such as a thirteenth-century location near Mt. Rokkō in Kobe.[43] In 1995, a wooden tablet in the *Nijō ōji* batch associated with the residence of Fujiwara no Maro, a famous victim of the 737 smallpox epidemic, contained an invocation to a nine-headed, single-tailed snake empowered to gobble up thousands of "fever demons," concluding with the formulaic *kyū kyū ritsuryō no gotoshi*.[44] Ancient residents of the archipelago undoubtedly learned about the myth and the formula from continentals, as references have been uncovered in Former Han, Tang, and Paekche texts.

Recently, Wakita Haruko authored a popular study of medieval Kyoto and Gion Shrine.[45] She makes three points about Heian-period "departed spirit" rituals and Gion that are central to the argument presented here. First, far from being merely an aristocratic superstition, *goryō-e* was also practiced in the countryside by the local populace. Toda Yoshimi was the first to make this point nearly thirty years ago by describing an entry in the aristocratic diary *Chūyūki*.[46] As Wakita notes, a similar tale is preserved in *Tales of Times Long Past (Konjaku monogatari)*. It portrays the locals as playing musical instruments, blowing whistles, and dancing "with no end to the insanity."[47] As with the archaeological evidence, Heian religion suggests a widespread popular concern with infectious outbreaks.[48]

Second, Wakita has investigated the origins and forms of the Gion myth of the "Bull-Headed King" and Somin Shōrai. While there is a Japanese tradition equating *Gozu tennō* with Susano-o no mikoto, a native Japanese god, Wakita argues that a bull-headed king with the power to loose epidemic visitations upon the populace was a foreign, and probably Indian, deity introduced to Japan via China.[49] Yet another scholar, Asaka Toshiki, attributes the epidemic god to peninsular (Silla) sources.[50] In either case, just as the god responsible for pestilence was a foreign deity, so an epidemic itself most often visited the Japanese archipelago from abroad during the Nara and Heian periods, à la McNeill's original thesis.

Third, Wakita has traced the development of "departed spirit" rites and Gion Shrine over the ancient and medieval periods.[51] During the ninth, tenth, and eleventh centuries, *goryō* rites were intimately linked to attempts to chase the epidemic god out of the city or nearby countryside. From about 1100, however, a Gion festival emerged and began to take on the form known today: Urbanites had carriages built and set a route through the streets of Kyoto. Moreover, the festival came to possess a more generalized meaning as a request for prosperity and the overall welfare of urbanites—not just as a way to escape pestilence. In my view, this change marked a decreasing fear of epidemics among Kyotoites; as various diseases became endemic in the city, foreign-borne infections ceased to have their previously deadly effect, and the Gion ritual became routinized.

During the middle and late Heian period, however, when "departed spirit" rites were most closely tied to virulent outbreaks of pestilence, cultural output was generally of a religious nature. To elaborate, this was the pessimistic age of millennial thought known as "The Coming of the Latter Day of the Buddhist Law" *(mappō jidai)*, a time when it was believed that it was all but impossible for a person to obtain salvation. One symbol of this intellectual world was *The Book of Illnesses (Yamai no sōshi)*, appearing in the mid-twelfth century and inspired by a sutra that listed the 404 sicknesses afflicting humanity.[52]

Also in the fine arts, scholars have recently begun to argue that the crafting of Buddhist iconography was closely tied to bouts of epidemics. A Japanese art historian has linked the creation and placement at Hōryūji of a statue of Kannon ("The Goddess of Mercy Who Saves the World") to the great epidemic of 735–37.[53] For the Heian period, Mimi Yiengpruksawan has noted that "thousands of statues were sponsored by royals and other aristocrats" between 990 and 1180.[54] While there are other explanations for the prodigious production during those years, Yiengpruksawan has asserted that disease "acted as an organizing principle for the body cultural." Sculptures became refined and elegant in reaction to the disfiguring effects of smallpox and measles—a real body polluted by illness. It is no accident that the plague affected European art, although in a different way, during the fourteenth and fifteenth centuries.[55]

The new data on death tolls, as well as testimony from archaeological and magico-religious perspectives, combine to underline McNeill's earlier seminal insight that the era from about 700 to 1150 or so was Japan's "age of microparasitism." Ravages of epidemic disease in turn had widespread ramifications, including substantial depopulation and its concomitant phenomena: field abandonment, village desertion, and a shrinking tax base.[56] Aristocrats of this age were aware of the problem; here is Miyoshi Kiyoyuki in his famous "Twelve-Article Opinion" (iken jūnikajō), written in 914:

> [I]n 660 . . . [t]he Emperor . . . tried to draft soldiers from a single village in Bingo; she obtained 20,000 fine troops.
> . . . Then in 765 and 766 . . . Kibi no Ason . . . tried to count the population of the village, [but] he found only 1,900+ male adults. [In the 860s], the late Minister of Population . . . Yasunori . . . was counting people. . . . [H]e searched for male adults and there were only 70+.
> When I, Kiyoyuki, went to my appointment [in 893] and researched the number of people in Bingo, I found only 2 old men, 4 adult males, and 3 teenage males. In 911, when the Vice-Governor of Bingo . . . returned to the capital, I asked him for the current population. He answered that no one was there any more.
> Respectfully counting up the years from 660 to 911, I see that there are only 252. How rapid the decline! If we extrapolate from this single village, we should come to understand the emptiness of the realm like the palm of my hand.[57]

Miyoshi was undoubtedly exaggerating. Recall, however, the figures inferred for the early eighth and mid-tenth centuries: about 5.8–6.4 million for the former and 4.4–5.6 million for the latter. Whether we rely upon these figures or Kitō's, it seems likely that the rate of population growth slowed markedly or was reversed between 700 and 950, even becoming negative for long stretches. For such a trend to hold sway in the absence of substantial out-migration or the end or decline of immigration without compensating changes in fertility or mortality, birth rates must have fallen, death rates risen, or some combination of the two must have been effected. The most plausible explanation for this phenomenon remains McNeill's hypothesis.

The acme of the second demographic cycle may well have been reached between 715 and 739, just as foreign-borne pestilence was becoming prevalent and lethal; it is no coincidence that in 723 narrative sources describe general overcrowding, which continued until the smallpox plague of 735–37 killed in its last year alone 15–44 percent of the adult population in an area ranging from northern Kyushu to eastern Honshu.[58] By 950 repeated ravages had taken their toll, probably reducing the archipelago's residents by as much as 30 percent from early eighth-century totals. By 1150, as the immunities of the insular populace increased, the number of inhabitants seems to have recovered, stabilizing at a level higher than in the depleted tenth century and at about the same level as in pre-epidemic days.

There is probably a measure of truth to the view that some substantial proportion of the population that had "disappeared" was simply no longer being recorded in the census. Yet a major factor in the atrophy of political systems of 702 (ritsuryō) and 900 (ōchō kokka) was the slight, or perhaps even precipitous, population decline between 700 and 1050. The major cause for this condition was the impact of foreign-borne infectious killers. The Chinese-style and classical Japanese states join European and Islamic societies from the mid-fourteenth to the end of the fifteenth century as historical monuments to the power of an ecological force beyond traditional human control—invisible but deadly microbes.

FAMINE

Despite its prominence in the debate over early modern population (1600–1868), until recently famine received virtually no attention for the ancient era. Fortunately, Saitō Osamu conducted a path-breaking study of famine in premodern times, and in another essay I focused upon crop failure and starvation in the years 670–1100.[59] (See Table 7.) This section summarizes the main findings of these two works in addition to analyzing subsistence crises between 1100 and 1150. (See Table 8.)

Unsurprisingly, famine stalked the archipelago frequently during this time. Until 900, harvest failure and starvation occurred more than once every three years on average; after that date, they were recorded much less often. While it is possible to maintain that the absence of subsistence crises represents a real trend toward a more plentiful diet, such a view does not jibe with abundant evidence of famine in the late Heian and medieval epochs. Both Saitō and I attribute the drop-off to a drastic decrease in records of all kinds during the tenth and early eleventh centuries. For example, the eighth century is documented in the massive twenty-five-volume Shōsōin collection and informative Shoku Nihongi, while the 800s include hundreds

Table 7. Famine Records, 670–1100

Period	General	Regional
670–700	2	2
700s	33	17
800s	26	27
900s	3	5
1000s	6	5
TOTAL	70	56

Source: The idea for this table originated with Saitō Osamu, "The Frequency of Famine as Demographic Correctives in the Japanese Past," 26, but I have evaluated the evidence on my own and the figures are mine. The weighted total is computed by attributing a value of 1 to an island-wide famine and .5 to a local incident.

Table 8. Famine Years, Their Extent and Causes, 1100–1150

Year	W/L*	CAUSE
1110	W	Cold, wet weather
1118	L	Same
1119	W	Drought and cold, wet weather
1131	W	Drought
1133	L	Same
1134	W	Cold, wet weather
1135	W	Cold, wet weather
1136	L	Unknown
1150	W	Cold, wet weather

*W stands for widespread and L for local. These data were taken from Sasaki Junnosuke, ed., *Nihon chūsei kōki kinsei shoki ni okeru kikin to sensō no kenkyū*, 14–18. I am grateful to Saitō Osamu for providing his original data as a guide. He relied upon Ogashima Minoru, ed., *Nihon saii shi*, 21; and Nishimura Makoto and Yoshikawa Ichirō, eds., *Nihon kyōkō shi kō*, 93–99. This table should be viewed in concert with Table 11.3 in William Wayne Farris, "Famine, Climate, and Farming in Ancient Japan."

of regulations (*kyaku*) and ordinances (*shiki*) and the continuation of the *Six National Histories*. By contrast, tenth-century documents extant in *Heian ibun* comprise only 5 percent of the total and there are no *National Histories;* the number of sources and extant documents increases slowly after 1100. In my view, the shortage of written materials between 900 and 1100 largely reflects the court's lack of interest in local affairs under the "dynastic state."

Untoward weather had a hand in almost all crop failures, with political causes such as war playing almost no role. Limiting the discussion to the period before 1100, we note that of the 125 famine years, 46 (36.8 percent) were associated with drought, while 33 (26.4 percent) were due to cold, damp summers, and the rest are unknown. More importantly, of the 71 years for which annalists chronicled widespread crop failures, more than half (38) arose from drought, 2.5 times the number (15) caused by cold, wet weather. Drought was particularly noticeable early on, with its incidence declining markedly in the era 1050–1100.

What can explain the seeming prevalence of dry weather? Modern patterns of precipitation do not seem to be related to the phenomenon. Based upon written and archaeological evidence from ancient Japan, it seems plausible that the islands were undergoing a marked wave of heat and drought varying by region. (See Table 9.) Moreover, comparative evidence from China, Western Europe, and possibly Central and North America suggests that northeast Asia, and probably the rest of the world, too, was experiencing "peak warm, dry events" between 670 and 1100. In other words, the hot, dry springs and summers were part of a larger worldwide trend, the causes of which are as yet poorly understood.

The high incidence of drought-induced harvest failures between 670 and 1100 was related to human activities in the archipelago in at least two ways. First, as the elite ordered and carried out monumental architecture in the Kinai, woodsmen stripped the timber cover, producing conditions ripe for drought and soil erosion in that densely settled and fiscally critical region. Second, most rice farmers watered their paddies naturally with rainfall from mountain run-off, and there were few or no irrigation facilities, such as "saucer ponds" or waterwheels, that could insulate crops from the vagaries of summer weather. Farmers rarely constructed elaborate irrigation works, which required huge inputs of labor not available in the Nara and Heian periods.

To combat famine in selected emergency years in the eighth and ninth centuries, the court encouraged peasants to plant wheat, barley, soybeans, millet, or buckwheat in the autumn but probably to little avail. While there is a chance that the commands were mere reiterations of nostrums from China, most scholars see them as the elite's attempt to cause peasants to

Table 9. Climatological Trends, 700–1200*

	Rain	Cold	Heat	Dryness	Total
Entries for 697–791	59	10	67	103	239
Percentile	25%	4.20%	28.00%	43.10%	
	Drought Index: 43		Wet, Cold Index: 29		
Entries for 1000–1099	52	24	35	55	166
Percentile	31.30%	14.50%	21.10%	33.10%	
	Drought Index: 33		Wet, Cold Index: 46		
Entries for 1100–1150	110	12	1	12	135
Percentile	80.00%	9.60%	0.80%	9.60%	
	Drought Index: 9.6		Wet, Cold Index: 89.6		
Entries for 1151–1200	124	12	42	72	250
Percentile	49.60%	4.80%	16.80%	28.80%	
	Drought Index: 28.8		Wet, Cold Index: 54.4		

*As revealed in Japanese sources. The ninth and tenth centuries were omitted because the former was included in William Wayne Farris, "Famine, Climate, and Farming in Ancient Japan," and there is not sufficient data for the latter. For the eighth century, I used the index to the *Shoku Nihongi*. For the eleventh and twelfth centuries, I relied exclusively upon Sasaki Junnosuke, ed., *Nihon chūsei kōki kinsei shoki ni okeru kikin to sensō no kenkyū*. In weighting the various entries, I counted snow, frost, and hail as 1 point each for moisture and cold; drought counted as 1 point each for both hot and dry; prayers for rain were entered as 1 point for dryness, and prayers to stop rain the opposite. Flood, great rain, violent rain, long rain, and even wind and rain all were considered as 1 point for dampness.

The drought index was computed by dividing the total number of references to dryness by n=total number of all climatological terms. The wet/cold index was calculated by dividing the total number of references to wet and cold by n.

engage in ad hoc double-cropping to tide them over until the next spring. In a related point, prices for rice over the famine year of 762 have been preserved in a document from the Shōsōin: They indicate that the ancient populace, like its counterpart in the medieval period, suffered from a "season of death" during the spring and summer when they had exhausted supplies of grain from the previous year and commoners were particularly likely to succumb to hunger or related maladies.[60]

These sundry pieces of evidence—the high percentage of famine years, the disproportionate incidence of drought-induced harvest failures, the repeated extraordinary orders to plant dry crops as a supplement to diet, and especially the price curve for 762—indicate that many persons led a hand-to-mouth existence of chronic or recurrent malnutrition. Taking an overview of court attempts to ameliorate these conditions, we notice that by the ninth century the central government had essentially run out of grain to succor the hungry and turned to wealthy individuals to carry the burden. It blamed its own local officials and they in turn berated farmers for the poor agricultural conditions. Gradually, the court focused its concern on keeping residents of the capital well-fed, letting provincials fend for themselves. Prayers and rituals seemed to be the only palliative within the court's grasp by 1100.

Turning to the era from 1100 to 1150, we observe that the occurrence of famine increases when compared to the record-poor tenth and eleventh centuries, there being nine years of shortage, six of them widespread. Most remarkable was the cause: Almost all the famines of this brief era were caused by unusually cold, damp weather; this was a great change from earlier centuries, when drought prevailed. According to most climatologists, the twelfth century was unusually hot and dry, but data taken from original sources indicate the opposite for the first five decades.[61] (See Table 9.) About 80 percent of references to weather relate to rain, with another 9.6 implying cold. Less than 1 percent of the entries discuss heat and less than 10 refer to drought. Minegishi Sumio has uncovered both written and archaeological evidence of volcanic activity at Mt. Fuji and Mt. Asama from the 1060s to 1110 or so, and perhaps the spewing of ash and smoke high into the atmosphere explains the prevalence of wet, cold climate and the famines caused by that weather over this period.[62] Climatological data in Table 8 also suggest that the first half of the twelfth century was colder than the second, and perhaps this presents a compromise solution. In any case, recorded famines were overwhelmingly caused by too much rain and cold. That was undoubtedly another cause for the severity of the influenza outbreaks.

While data are sparse, it may be instructive to describe a twelfth-century crop failure.[63] During 1118–19, the crisis seems to have been limited to Kyoto at first, although we cannot be sure. Once again it was cold and wet in the early summer, and the realm's wheat crop suffered damage. In the early fall, Kyotoites were in desperate straits, and Retired Emperor Shirakawa opened the city's granaries to succor the hungry. Early in 1119, an epidemic combined with the famine led Fujiwara no Munetada to comment that this year the realm has numerous dead, and added to that there are starving folk, too. In the capital, those who commit arson and robbery are extremely numerous every night. Superiors ask no questions and inferiors pretend as though nothing happened. It is truly frightening. The hearts of underlings cannot be respected.

Later Munetada added murder to the list of criminal offenses. As in the case of the pestilence in 1134–35, famine and infectious outbreak resulted in violence and social disintegration.

Returning to the big picture, we might make two other generalizations about famine in Japan to 1150. First, while hunger was a constant companion for many, and a dire threat under the worst circumstances, it was probably not as deadly as disease. Figures for famine mortality in the ancient age are difficult to come by, but victims typically numbered in the hundreds and occasionally thousands. In 790, for example, provincial government records state that 88,000 persons were starving in Kyushu; if we apply Sawada's estimate for the island's population (664,400), then about 13 percent were going hungry. In 854 similar reports speak of 19,000 residents of Dewa, or about 32.7 percent of its inhabitants according to Sawada, as receiving tax relief in the face of crop failure. Neither figure should be equated with mortality, but they imply that life was hard and that famine contributed to some degree to the harsh demographic regime of the period.

Second, while crop failure probably did not claim as many lives as pestilence, the two killers often acted in tandem. For the years 697–758 and 806–87, correlation coefficients are .88 and .79, respectively.[64] We may view this relationship in many ways: Possibly a disease outbreak weakened the populace and led to the inability to labor daily in the fields, which enhanced the likelihood of harvest failure. Or famine may have reduced immunity to infections. Or some epidemics (kieki) may have actually been acute diarrhea, a condition apparent in starvation victims immediately before death. In any case, it seems likely that harvest failure and pestilence went hand-in-hand.

In essence, famine seems to have comprised a critical secondary variable driving up death rates and hampering fertility in the epoch 670–1150. It also suggests the primitive level of agriculture, especially rice cultivation, at this stage. It is well to remember that not only were irrigation works few and unreliable, but most of the agronomic techniques that eventually made farming lucrative—practices such as annual double-cropping, the planting of Champa rice, and the regularized application of fertilizers such as manures and night soil—had not yet appeared. These points represent one more reason to view optimistic evaluations of middle and late Heian agriculture with a doubtful eye and to accept the population totals and interpretation adduced thus far.

CHAPTER 2

WAR AND POLITICAL INSTABILITY

Many works have described the major conflicts over the Nara-Heian period, and while violence was not rare, especially as greater social problems emerged after 900, in general the political system was relatively stable.[65] The great wars—the expeditions to northeastern Honshu from 774 to 812, Taira no Masakado's and Fujiwara Sumitomo's rebellions of 935–41, Taira no Tadatsune's revolt occurring during 1028–32, and the eleventh-century battles in Mutsu (1051–62; 1083–87)—certainly caused their share of death and destruction, as troops burned hamlets and fields, requisitioned grain, animals, and supplies, and impressed peasants into service.[66] Except for the giant campaigns waged in the eighth century, however, military forces remained small and were not so capable of disrupting rural life as in later centuries. Moreover, hostilities were limited to a single region, usually either the Kanto or northeastern Honshu. As Mikael Adolphson has shown, religious devotees could wreak destruction and death in the Kinai, especially beginning in the late eleventh century, but these too seem to have had little impact on the general populace.[67] It appears safe to say that until 1150 war and violence were a distant third among the causes of mortality and infertility, with both disease and famine producing harsher effects. The relatively mild consequences of human violence fits the conventional wisdom that people in the premodern era were not nearly so good at killing each other as were natural forces such as disease and inclement weather.

A further consideration regarding political stability is the flow of taxes to officialdom. All indications are that nonpayment of revenues became an unremitting concern for the government from the late eighth century. Almost forty years ago, Hayakawa Shōhachi showed how the court first suffered from a shortfall in income, then practiced retrenchment around 800, and finally spent the ninth and early tenth centuries cannibalizing the tax bases of provincial governments.[68] During the era from the early 900s until 1050 or so, custodial governors served as tax-farmers to supply the capital elite; even then the court sold offices and aristocratic rank to raise sufficient funds.[69] The inadequacy of official receipts is a constant refrain in the Heian volume of *The Cambridge History of Japan*. Phrases such as "further contraction of the government's fiscal base," "a persistent insufficiency of income," "revenues continued to decline in quality and quantity," "a contraction of government revenues," "deliveries of handicraft taxes were late, incomplete, and of poor quality," recur.[70] The most straightforward interpretation regarding revenue flows to the capital over the period 700–1050, and the one that matches the hypothesis advanced here, is that demographic loss led to shrinkage in the tax base. Fewer producers meant less revenue—at least until the population began to grow and the *shōen-kokugaryō* system came into being and eventually stabilized the situation beginning in the late eleventh century.

Scholars have traditionally advanced two other views to explain the shortfall. The first and oldest maintains that so many large tracts of land had been converted to nontaxable estates by the 900s that revenues declined.[71] The problem with this view is that estates of the ninth, tenth, and early eleventh centuries were taxable; most estates of that era were small and impermanent; and *shōen* never amounted to much more than 50 percent of Japan's arable—even in their heyday, the 1100s and 1200s. The true age of estate formation took place in the second half of the eleventh and twelfth centuries, when local elites brought formerly abandoned paddies and dry fields back into production and commended those lands to civil aristocrats and religious institutions, thereby avoiding tax obligations.

The second, more sophisticated explanation is that local elites were holding back the surplus and thus becoming wealthier—and in the process reduced the amount of taxes going to the capital aristocracy and religious institutions.[72] Although solid evidence on the issue is thin, it is worthwhile keeping two considerations in mind: The number of "local notables" seems to have changed little from the early 700s until 1250, continually ranging between two and three thousand individuals; and district magistrates in the 700s appear to have collected at least as generous perquisites as warriors in the 1100s.[73] Admittedly, the pertinent information comes down to historians in a fragmentary and therefore debatable form, but it seems wise to question how seriously local abuses hurt the treasury.

Notes

1. Fukuhara Eitarō, "Tenpyō kyūnen no ekibyō ryūkō to sono seijiteki eikyō ni tsuite," *Kōbe Yamate daigaku kankyō bunka kenkyō jo kiyō* 4 (2000): 27–39; "Futatabi Tenpyō kyūnen no ekibyō ryūkō to sono eikyō ni tsuite," in Hashimoto Masayoshi, ed., *Kankyō rekishi no shiza* (Iwata shoin, 2002), 75–106. In the second article, Fukuhara utilizes the rice loan reports analyzed in William Wayne Farris, *Population, Disease and Land in Early Japan, 645-900* (Council on East Asian Studies, Harvard University, 1985), 64–67, to obtain his general mortality figure. For the record, I find Fukuhara's mortality estimate to be somewhat too high.

Another indirect benefit of Fukuhara's tabulation of all epidemics noted in *Shoku Nihongi* is that he has confirmed what other scholars (such as Tamura Noriyoshi) had long suspected was a unique "seasonality of death" for infection-riddled societies. To wit, Fukuhara showed that more than 76 percent of all pestilence racked Japan between the third and eighth months—in other words, from late spring to early autumn. Tamura Noriyoshi ("Chūsei jin no 'shi' to 'sei'" *Nihon shi kenkyū* 388 [December 1994]: 112–14) first noticed this so-called "inverted-V" mortality curve. See the discussion of famine below.

Another recent treatment of a document relating to the 735–37 epidemic may be found in Maruyama Yumiko, "Kodai no tennō to byōsha," in *Iwanami kōza Tennō to ōken o kangaeru 8 Kosumorojii to shintai* (Iwanami shoten, 2002), 209–12. Maruyama argues that the Council of State order dated to 737, which describes the symptoms and remedies for the disease, was not drawn from Chinese medicine and was preserved to aid future generations in fighting smallpox. She also asserts that the order was posted on placards all over Japan, attesting to the widespread dispersion of the virus. For a translation of the order, see Farris, *Population, Disease, and Land*, 60–61.

2. Fujikawa Yū, *Nihon shippei shi* (Heibon sha, 1969); Hattori Toshirō, *Heian jidai igaku no kenkyū* (Kuwana bunsei dō, 1955).

3.*Nihon sandai jitsuroku* (Yoshikawa kōbunkan, 1934), Jōgan 12/8/5, 276.

4. Fujikawa, *Nihon shippei shi*, 29–30; *Nihon kiryaku* (Yoshikawa kōbunkan, 1929), Shōryaku 4/6/20, 175; Shōryaku 5/3/26, 177; Shōryaku 5/4/10, 177; Shōryaku 5/4/24, 177; Shōryaku 5/4/25, 177; Shōryaku 5/4/27, 177; Shōryaku 5/4/28, 177; Shōryaku 5/5/3, 178; Shōryaku 5/5/11, 178; Shōryaku 5/5/16, 178; Shōryaku 5/5/26, 178; Shōryaku 5/6/27, 178; Shōryaku 5/7/21, 178; Shōryaku 5/8/8, 178; Shōryaku 5/8/10, 178; Shōryaku 5/12, 179; Chōtoku 1/2/9, 181; Chōtoku 1/2/22, 181; Chōtoku 1/4/27, 182; Chōtoku 1/5/29, 182; Chōtoku 1/7, 183; *Hyakuren shō* (Yoshikawa kōbunkan, 1929), Shōryaku 5/*kono toshi no jō*, 8; *Ruijū fusen shō* (Yoshikawa kōbunkan, 1933), 81–82.

5. Mochida Yasuhiko, "Nara chō kizoku no ninzu henka ni tsuite," *Gakushūin shigaku* 15 (January 1979): 17–35.

6. Tsuchida Naoshige, *Nihon no rekishi 5 Ōchō no kizoku* (Chūō kōron sha, 1965), 394.

7. *Heian ibun*, edited by Takeuchi Rizō (Tokyo dō, 1965), 2:609.

8. Ibid., 2:656.

9. Ibid., 3:1100.

10. Ibid., 2:743.

11. *A Tale of Flowering Fortunes*, translated by William McCullough and Helen McCullough (Stanford: Stanford University Press, 1980), 112. Regarding other epidemics in the late tenth and eleventh centuries, see also pp. 168–83 and 211–16 (the years 994–98); pp. 517–29 (the years 1019–22); and pp. 665–96 (the years 1025–26).

12. Ibid., 520.

13. My description of this epidemic and its effects follows Gomi Fumihiko, *Insei ki shakai no kenkyū* (Yamakawa shuppan sha, 1984), 291–97.

14. *Chūyūki*, VI (Kyoto: Rinsen shoten, 1965), Chōshō 1/Int. 4/16, 310; *Hyakuren shō*, Chōshō 1/*kotoshi no jō*, 59; *Chūyūki*, VII, Chōshō 3/10/25, 115; Chōshō 3/Int. 12/30, p. 122; *Hōen* 1/5/5, 147; *Hyakuren shō*, Chōshō 1/5, 59; Hōen 1/7/1, 60.

15. A second wave of influenza was at least as bad as the first, although it is not so well recorded. Court annals stated that "among the aristocrat and servile as well as high and low, none was spared. The aged died in great numbers and commoners died a pitiful death. In recent years this has been the worst outbreak of the disease" (*Honchō seiki* [Yoshikawa kōbunkan, 1964], Kyūan 6/10/26, 731; Kyūan 6/11/28, 734). In the next month, the same annal stated that there was no one who did not become ill with the affliction; the imperial palace and offices were empty. Little did residents know that even those who had survived the outbreak were not immune to a new strain of the same virus poised to attack after 1150.

Other than these named diseases, early twelfth-century annalists were typically content with the general term for "epidemic," either not knowing or caring about the particular affliction. One unnamed outbreak that seems to have been especially virulent occurred in 1105–6, when Fujiwara no Munetada, author of the diary *Chūyūki*, wrote for 1105 that "recently the realm *(tenka)* is unsettled. Sick persons beyond counting litter the sides of the roads. Along the river banks the dead are everywhere" *(Chūyūki*, III, Chōji 2/4/24, 40). In the next year the epidemic did not abate, and Munetada again noted that the dead were innumerable, filling up roads and riverbanks: "Recently corpses are beginning to pile up; this can really be called a major pestilence *(daieki)*" (Kashō 1/6/5, 123). He repeated the lament again the next year; the diarist of the *Eishō ki*, Fujiwara no Tametaka, described a ritual to purify the four corners and boundaries of Kyoto (Kashō 2/3/30, 203; *Eishō ki* [Kyoto: Rinsen shoten, 1965], Kashō 1/4/12, 24).

In 1154 people in the capital reported "the empty child illness" *(munashiki ko no yamai)*, apparently a scourge of infants (Hattori, *Heian jidai igaku no kenkyū*, 207).

16. Kaneko Hiroyuki, ed., *Ritsuryō ki saishi ibutsu shūsei* (Nara kokuritsu bunka zai kenkyū jo, 1988); "Saishi kankei ibutsu shutsudo chi chimei hyō," *Kokuritsu rekishi minzoku hakubutsukan kenkyū hōkoku fuhen* 7 (March 1985): 1–805; "Kodai no mokusei mozō hin," *Nara kokuritsu bunka zai kenkyū jo kenkyū ronshū* 6 (March 1980): 5–28; "Nihon ni okeru hitogata no kigen," in Fukunaga Mitsuji, ed., *Dōkyō to higashi Ajia* (Jinbun shoin, 1989), 37–54; "Mokusei mozō hin," in *Shintō kōkogaku kōza* (Yūzan kaku, 1981), 3:79–87; and below.

17. Kaneko Hiroyuki, "Tojin no seishin seikatsu," in Kishi Toshio, ed., *Nihon no kodai* 9 *Tojō no seitai* (Chūō kōron sha, 1987), 356.

18. Ibid., 347–49.

19. On these artifacts, see Kaneko, "Seishin seikatsu," 347–56; "Tojō to saishi," in Oda Fujio, ed., *Okinoshima to kodai saishi* (Yoshikawa kōbunkan, 1988), 201–4, 212, 213–16; "Heijō kyō to saijō," *Kokuritsu rekishi minzoku hakubutsukan kenkyū hōkoku* 7 (March 1985): 246–48.

20. The artifacts were found lying in a ditch parallel to the main east-west road at Nara, Second Rank Great Avenue *(nijō ōji)*.

21. Kaneko, "Seishin seikatsu," 350–51.

22. Kaneko, "Tojō to saishi," 205–6.

23. *Engi jingi shiki, Chūgū miagata sai no jō* (Yoshikawa kōbunkan, 1977), 27–28; *Kojitsu sōsho* 6 *Saikyūki*, 1:35. Also note *Engi-shiki: Procedures of the Engi Era*, translated by Felicia Bock (Sophia University, 1970), 83–86.

24. *Nihon kiryaku*, Shōryaku 5/6/27, 178.

25. Kaneko, "Tojō to saishi," 216–20; "Heijō kyō to saijō," 238.

26. Mizuno Masayoshi, "Uma-uma-uma: sono katari no kōkogaku," *Bunka zai gakuhō* 2 (March 1983): 23–43; Kaneko, "Heijō kyō to saijō," 264–66; Kuroda Hideo, *Nihon chūsei kaihatsu shi no kenkyū* (Azekura shobō, 1984), 463–65.

27. Kaneko, "Tojō to saishi," 206.

28. Ibid., pp. 220–22.

29. Kaneko, "Heijō kyō to saijō," 267; "Tojō to saishi," 206–7.

30. On foreign dignitaries, see *Jingi-ryō no shūge, Dōkyō sai no jō*, 196; on boundaries, see Sekiguchi Yasuyuki, "Ekishin saishi chi to shūyō kōtsū ro," *Chiri gakuhō* 28 (1992): 111–28.

31. Kaneko, "Tojō to saishi," 198–201; "Kodai no mokusei mozō hin," 17–26.

CHAPTER 2

32. Izumi Takeshi, "Ritsuryō saishi ron ichi shiten," in Fukunaga, ed., *Dōkyō to higashi Ajia*, 55–99.

33. Yi Hyŏn-suk, "Silla t'ongilgi chŏnyombyŏng ui yuhaeng gwa taeŭngchaek," *Hanguk kodae sa yŏn'gu* 31 (September 2003): 209–56; "7 segi Silla t'ongil chŏnchaeng gwa chŏnyombyŏng," *Yŏksa hwa hyŏnsil* 47 (March 2003): 89–147.

34. Neil McMullin, "On Placating the Gods and Pacifying the Populace: The Case of the Gion *Goryō* Cult," *History of Religions* 27 (February 1988): 270–93; Alan Grapard, "Religious Practices," in Donald H. Shively and William McCullough, eds., *The Cambridge History of Japan* (Cambridge: Cambridge University Press, 1999), 2:517–75. Shinto also played a role in the *goryō* cult; see Fabio Rambelli and Mark Teeuwen, eds., "Introduction: Combinatory Religion and the *Honji suijaku* Paradigm in Pre-Modern Japan," in their *Buddhas and Kami in Japan* (London: Routledge Curzon, 2003), 26–30; and Irene Lin, "From Thunder Child to Dharma-Protector: Dōjō hōshi and the Buddhist Appropriation of Japanese Local Deities," in Rambelli and Teeuwen, eds., *Buddhas and Kami in Japan*, 59–76. Even Amaterasu eventually was held responsible for the onset of pathogenic outbreaks; see Mark Teeuwen, "The Creation of a *Honji suijaku* Deity: Amaterasu as the Judge of the Dead," in Rambelli and Teeuwen, eds, *Buddhas and Kami in Japan*, 122–38.

35. On this rite, there are many good Japanese articles. To cite a few: Shibata Minoru, *Goryō shinkō* (Yūzan kaku, 1984); Ōshima Tatehiko, *Ekishin to sono shūhen* (Iwasaki bijutsu sha, 1985); Nishiyama Ryōhei, "Goryō shinkō ron," in *Iwanami kōza Nihon tsūshi 5 Kodai 4* (Iwanami shoten, 1993), 333–46; Sakō Nobuyuki, "Ekishin shinkō no seiritsu," in *Mura kōzō to takai kan* (Yūzan kaku, 1985), 113–36; Ōno Tsutomu, "Heian jidai no goryō shisō," *Nihon rekishi* 114 (December 1957): 41–49; Saeki Arikiyo, *Nihon kodai no seiji to shakai* (Yoshikawa kōbunkan, 1970), 225–66; Iwaki Takatoshi, "Goryō-e no hassei," in *Kokushi ronshū* (Dokushi kai, 1959), 1:443–58; Nishio Masato, "Ekibyō kami shinkō no seiritsu," in *Minzoku shūkyō 3 Ōken to shamanizumu* (Tokyo dō, 1990), 255–80; Matsumae Takeshi, "Gion gozu tennō sha no sōken to tennō shinkō no genryū," in *Kodai gaku sōron* (Tsunoda Bun'ei sensei koki kinen jigyō kai, 1983), 435–46; Takatori Masao, "Goryō shinkō o rikai suru tame ni," *Shisō* 38 (December 1980): 80–95; Kuroda, *Nihon chūsei kaihatsu shi*, 406–65; and below. *Kokubungaku: Kaishaku to kanshō* devoted an entire issue to the topic: "Tokushū: kodai ni miru goryō to shinbutsu shūgō," 36 (March 1999). For an even more recent treatment repeating many of the themes adumbrated in the text, see Yamamoto Kōji, "Tennō to shukusai," in *Iwanami kōza Tennō to ōken o kangaeru 8 Kosumorojii to shintai*, 153–76.

36. State-supported Shinto also played a role in fighting epidemics; see Nelly Naumann, "The State Cult of the Nara and Early Heian Periods," in John Breen and Mark Teeuwen, eds., *Shinto in History: Ways of the Kami* (Honolulu: University of Hawai'i Press, 2000), 53–62.

37. *Nihon sandai jitsuroku* (Yoshikawa kōbunkan, 1934), Jōgan 5/5/20, 112–13; Naga Yōichi, "Jōgan gonen goryō e ni tsuite no ichi shiron," *Kyushu shigaku* 5 (August 1957): 17–26.

38. Grapard, "Religious Practices," 2:559.

39. Asaka Toshiki, "Kodai no Hokuriku dō ni okeru kanshin shinkō," *Nihon kai bunka* 6 (March 1979): 1–29.

40. Iwaki, "Goryō-e no hassei," 443.

41. McMullin, "On Placating the Gods," 270–71; Wakita Haruko, *Chūsei Kyoto to Gion matsuri* (Chūkō shinsho, 1999), 67–112.

42. McMullin, "On Placating the Gods," 274.

43. See, for example, Sakaguchi Toshiyuki, "Magarigawa iseki," *Mokkan kenkyū* 9 (1987): 29; Mori Kōzō, "Ōzone iseki," *Mokkan kenkyū* 12 (1990): 86. Also note Maeda Ryōichi, "'Kyūkyū ritsuryō no gotoshi' o saguru," in Fukunaga, ed., *Dōkyō to higashi Ajia*, 101–26.

44. For the text of this tablet and a sound interpretation, see Ogata Tetsushi, "Nijō ōji mokkan no jumon," *Mokkan kenkyū* 18 (1996): 246. Also note Wada Atsumu, "Nansan no kyūtō ryū," in *Nihon kokka no shiteki tokushitsu kodai chūsei* (Shibunkaku shuppan, 1997), 287–310.

45. Wakita, *Chūsei Kyoto to Gion*, 2–7, 31–44.

46. Toda Yoshimi, "Shōen taisei kakuritsu ki no shūkyōteki minshū undō," *Rekishigaku kenkyū* 378 (November 1971): 8–15. See also Kuroda, *Nihon chūsei kaihatsu shi*, 458–74. Also note Yoshii Toshiyuki ("Yamato no kuni Ochi no kohori Ryōanji to goryō jinja," *Nihon shūkyō bunka shi kenkyū* 5 [2001]: 113–41), who counts twenty-one sites in one small section of Yamato where some type of "departed spirit" rite was observed. Many of these shrines, however, date from the medieval and early modern periods.

47. *Konjaku monogatari shū*, edited by Yamada Takao et al. (Iwanami shoten, 1961), 5:68–71; Wakita, *Chūsei Kyoto to Gion*, 4.

48. Along these lines, Tokunaga Chikako ("Shugendō seiritsu no shiteki zentei," *Shirin* 84 [January 2001]: 97–123) argues that the Buddhist tradition of monks wandering through the mountains to obtain the ability to perform magical feats *(shugen dō)* got its start in the tenth century, when purified, learned ascetics *(kensha)*, primarily of the Tendai sect, moved among the populace dispensing "cures" *(noroi)*.

49. Wakita, *Chūsei Kyoto to Gion*, 96–112.

50. Asaka, "Kodai no Hokuriku dō ni okeru kanshin shinkō," 14–22.

51. Wakita, *Chūsei Kyoto to Gion*, 16–50.

52. Komatsu Shigemi, ed., *Nihon no emaki*, vol. 7, 138–39. Also note the references to epidemics in other religious texts of this time, such as *Miraculous Tales of the Lotus Sutra from Ancient Japan*, translated by Yoshiko Dykstra (Osaka: Kansai University of Foreign Studies, 1983), 8; and the rise of a Shingon esoteric rite for healing that became popular at this time; see Pamela Winfield, "Curing with *Kaji*: Healing and Esoteric Empowerment in Japan," *Japanese Journal of Religious Studies* 32 (2005): 115–23.

53. Kondō Ariyoshi, "Hōryūji tōin no Kuse Kannon zō anchi ni tsuite," *Nihon rekishi* 653 (October 2002): 1–17.

54. Mimi Yiengpruksawan, "The Visual Ideology of Buddhist Sculpture in the Late Heian Period as Configured by Epidemic and Disease," in *Iconography and Style in Buddhist Art Historical Studies* (Kobe: Kobe University, 1995), 69–79. Inaki Yoshikazu ("'Wayō' bijutsu to Heian jidai no shūkyō kan," *Nihon shūkyō bunka shi kenkyū* 6.1 [2002]: 31–45) links a change in iconographic style at this time to aristocratic magical attempts to ward off disease and increase life expectancy.

55. Robert Gottfried, *The Black Death* (New York: The Free Press, 1983), 91–93.

56. On land abandonment and deserted villages, see Yoshida Takashi, "Ritsuryō sei to sonraku," in *Iwanami kōza Nihon rekishi* 3 *Kodai* 3 (Iwanami shoten, 1976), 158, 170–71. On the shrinking tax base, see William McCullough, "The Heian Court, 794–1070," in McCullough and Shively, eds., *The Cambridge History of Japan*, 2:38, 44, 72. These points will be illustrated further below.

57. Miyoshi Kiyoyuki, *Iken jūnikajō*, in Takeuchi Rizō et al., eds., *Nihon shisō taikei*

8, *Kodai seiji shakai shisō*, 78–79. Of course, Miyoshi refers to an event (the death of Emperor Saimei in Kyushu) and a reign period (Engi 11) in his text. He probably consulted court annals to arrive at such a precise calculation of time.

58. Farris, *Population, Disease, and Land*, 64–69.

59. Saitō Osamu, "The Frequency of Famines as Demographic Correctives in the Japanese Past," *The Institute of Economic Research, Hitotsubashi University: Discussion Paper Series A* 386 (January 2000): 1–32; William Wayne Farris, "Famine, Climate, and Farming in Early Japan, 670–1100," in Mikael Adolphson, Edward Kamens, and Stacie Matsumoto, eds., *Heian Japan, Centers and Peripheries* (Honolulu: University of Hawai'i Press, 2007), 275–304.

60. On these orders, see Isogai Fujio, *Chūsei no nōgyō to kikō* (Yoshikawa kōbunkan, 2002), 17–56. The reader should recall that epidemics also produced their own unique "season of death," lasting from the third through the eighth months (see Note 1). Because the populace of the ancient age suffered from both pestilence and famine, a mortality curve would probably show heightened death rates for the first through eighth months, concentrating in the summer months when commoners might have been subject to a "double dose" of starvation and disease. The fall and winter months would seem to be the "safest" seasons.

61. Isogai Fujio, "Nihon chūsei shi kenkyū to kikō hendō ron," *Nihon shi kenkyū* 388 (December 1994): 25–49, cites all the prevailing theories. Isogai recently reiterated his views in *Chūsei no nōgyō to kikō*, 193–277. For the raw data on which I based my calculations, see Note 63.

62. Minegishi Sumio, *Chūsei saigai senran no shakai shi* (Yoshikawa kōbunkan, 2001), 43–63. Of course, there are a whole host of imponderables such as wind direction, the amount of ash ejected, the length of the volcanic activity, etc.

63. The information in this paragraph is based on Sasaki Junnosuke, ed., *Nihon chūsei kōki kinsei shoki ni okeru kikin to sensō no kenkyū* (Waseda daigaku kyōiku gakubu, 2000), 14–18; Nishimura Makoto and Yoshikawa Ichirō, eds., *Nihon kyōkō shi kō* (Maruzen, 1936), 93–99. The quotation appears in *Chūyūki*, 5, Gen'ei 2/2/18, 113.

64. These coefficients were tabulated from Tsuguda Yoshiharu, "Shōzui saii kō," *Senshū shigaku* 23 (April 1991): 50–71. The weaker correlation for 759–805 could be due to the fragmentary sources of that era or some other bias in the way famines and epidemics were reported or recorded.

65. On war, see William Wayne Farris, *Heavenly Warriors: The Evolution of Japan's Military, 500–1300* (Council on East Asian Studies, Harvard University, 1992), 81–162; 192–200; 223–40. Note Karl Friday, *Hired Swords: The Rise of Private Warrior Power in Early Japan* (Stanford: Stanford University Press, 1992); "Pushing Beyond the Pale: The Yamato Conquest of the *Emishi* and Northern Japan," *Journal of Japanese Studies* 23 (winter 1997): 1–24; *Samurai, Warfare, and the State in Early Medieval Japan* (New York and London: Routledge Press, 2004), 130; and Paul Varley, *Warriors of Japan as Portrayed in the War Tales* (Honolulu: University of Hawai'i Press, 1994), 1–77.

66. The works cited in Note 65 relate the best descriptions of war, but it is generally difficult to obtain a precise idea of mortality and destruction. Death rates among combatants seem to have been low, but conflict could cause considerable damage to local farmers, as in the case of Tadatsune's revolt and the expeditions against the "barbarians" in the late eighth century. Both famine and epidemic occasionally bore some relationship to war. For the havoc that warriors could wreak upon the general populace even during peacetime, see Yasuda Motohisa, *Nihon shoki hōken sei no kiso*

kenkyū (Yamakawa shuppan, 1976), 185–200. For a brief treatment in English, see Farris, *Heavenly Warriors*, 217–20.

67. Mikael S. Adolphson, *The Gates of Power: Monks, Courtiers, and Warriors in Pre-Modern Japan* (Honolulu: University of Hawai'i Press, 2000), 75–184, examines the most well-documented incidents.

68. Hayakawa Shōhachi, "Ritsuryō zaisei no kōzō to sono henshitsu," in Iyanaga Teizō, ed., *Nihon keizai shi taikei 1 Kodai* (Tokyo daigaku shuppan kai, 1965), 259–80.

69. Uejima Susumu, "Jōkō sei no tenkai," *Shirin* 75 (July 1992): 74–113

70. The following quotations appear in McCullough, "The Heian Court," 38, 44, 72; Dana Morris, "Land and Society," in Shively and McCullough, eds., *The Cambridge History of Japan*, 2:206–8.

71. For example, see George Sansom, *Japan: A Short Cultural History to 1334* (Stanford: Stanford University Press, 1958) 82–196; Edwin O. Reischauer, John Fairbank, and Albert Craig, *East Asia: Tradition and Transformation* (Boston: Houghton Mifflin, 1989), 324–57; John Hall, *Government and Local Power in Japan 500 to 1700* (Princeton: Princeton University, 1966), 99–128. For evidence that the tenth and eleventh centuries witnessed the nadir, and not acme, of estate formation, see Uno Takao, *Shōen no kōkogaku* (Aoki shoten, 2001), 63–68. Also see Note 56.

72. The most recent assertion of this interpretation is to be found in Morris, "Land and Society," 224–35.

73. Farris, *Heavenly Warriors*, 104–13; 335–52; 355–80.

CHAPTER 3

Background Factors

This work now turns from variables such as epidemics and wars that have a direct bearing on mortality and fertility to indirect or background components that also indicate a static population from 700 to 1150. The first of these measures concerns the economy, including agriculture, the labor market and industry, and trade and urbanization. Among these, farming is perhaps most crucial because it helps to determine the amount of food. In dealing with agriculture, I will first touch upon land use until about 1050, then proceed to middle Heian technological change, and finally deal with the late Heian period and the so-called "age of widespread land clearance." Some reflections on settlement patterns and migration will round out this section.

AGRICULTURE AND SETTLEMENT

The frequency with which peasants crop potential farmland is critical because it affects the quantity and quality of the food supply, which can play a large role in a populace's fertility and longevity. During the Nara and Heian eras, it has become clear that the agrarian regime was generally extensive and may best be envisioned as "a repeated cycle of land clearance and abandonment"—to borrow Yoshida Takashi's apt phrase.[1] Or, to cite Tsude Hiroshi, it is likely that any real increase in arable or improvements in agrarian technology took place prior to 700, before officials kept written documents or such records were extant. After 700, land tenure and taxation became central concerns for a record-keeping court, as the area under cultivation reached an optimal size given the population density and level of agricultural technology.[2]

To elaborate, as early as the 1960s Harashima Reiji analyzed eighth-century documents to show that abandoned fields comprised 12–44 percent of arable lands.[3] For the early and middle Heian eras, Cornelius Kiley recently conducted a detailed examination of the provincial system for reporting uncultivated fields (*fukanden den*) to the central government.[4] In Kiley's words, "[r]eported acreage totals of uncultivatable fields had a pronounced tendency to increase" during the ninth and tenth centuries. To be sure, official and peasant chicanery may have often been part of the problem, as Kiley maintains, but even the appearance of such a reporting system, by which the court required local officials to announce every year how much land tillers were farming and under which officials assumed that 10 percent of all fields were usually barren, suggests a sizable degree of rural depopulation. To quote Kiley again, "conflicts over . . . [uncultivated fields] and damage reports . . . preoccupied the officials of the early Heian era." One wonders if the 25 percent figure deducted from the total listed in *Wamyō shō* may not have actually underestimated the unproductive land of the ninth, tenth, and early eleventh centuries.[5]

Mid-Heian Technological Change

How did the existence of more abandoned fields and a decline in population density around 950 affect agricultural technology? In general, agrarian regimes of the ninth, tenth, and eleventh centuries remained diverse and protean. Cultivators practiced two types of wet-rice farming: one relying on artificial irrigation, the other on rainfall, often in the form of run-off from mountains into small paddies located in valleys. Dry farming was common, although probably not as productive as even poor rice paddies at least until the late eleventh century. Slash-and-burn cropping and a whole host of nonagricultural livelihoods, including fishing, hunting, and gathering, helped to sustain the population.

The one major technological innovation that did occur—the development and diffusion of the plow and draft animals—took place precisely because of the shortage of farmhands and the abundance of erstwhile fields turned to grazing. Following in the footsteps of Furushima Toshio, the dean of Japanese agrarian historians, Dana Morris stressed this invention in his essay in *The Cambridge History of Japan*.[6] The weakness in his argument was that the evidence—a citation in the encyclopedic *Wamyō shō*, a mention for the imperial kitchen gardens in *The Ordinances of Engi*, and references in three literary works—is slender.[7] Moreover, the Heian plow, which Morris correctly termed a "moldboard" plow, did not achieve the deep tillage of the large, heavy wheeled implement drawn by four oxen during Western Europe's "age of widespread land clearance" (about 800–1200 CE). Experiments performed with Japanese plows utilizing small moldboards to turn the soil indicate that they cut the earth only about 3 centimeters deeper than a peasant's hoe or spade.[8] This conclusion fits with the kind of plowing necessary for rice paddies, which contain pans that planters should not pierce lest they start leaking.[9]

Before we dismiss the Heian ox-drawn plow too quickly, however, it should be noted that some Japanese historians have uncovered facts that corroborate Morris' emphasis on the plow, if not his conception of its shape and use.[10] Kōno Michiaki, for example, has asserted that both the plow and especially draft animals became much more prominent in Japanese farming—both irrigated and unirrigated—beginning in the middle Heian era. His chief sources for this view are archaeological and visual data, which reveal a new type of dual harness placed over the neck and shoulders of the beast. (See Figure 5.) Kōno indicates that wealthy cultivators, known in the

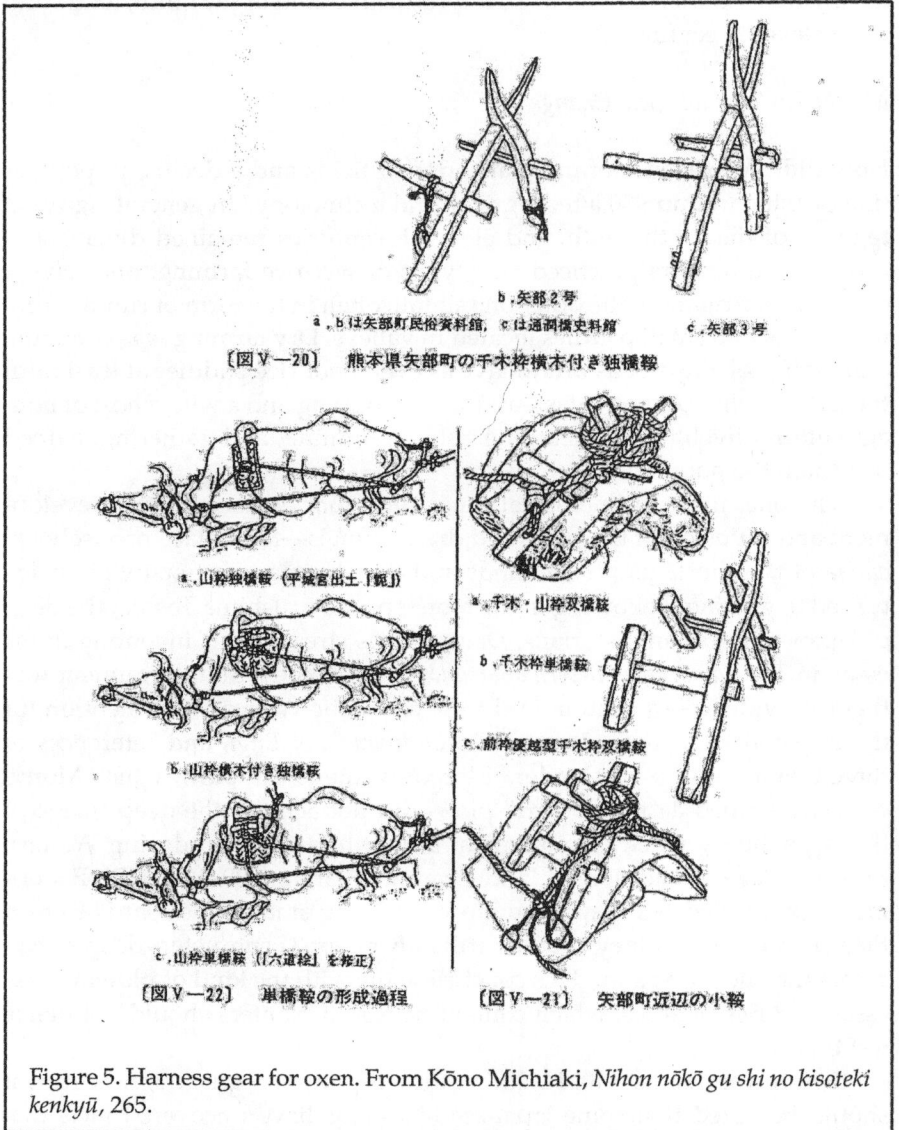

Figure 5. Harness gear for oxen. From Kōno Michiaki, *Nihon nōkō gu shi no kisoteki kenkyū*, 265.

records as *tato* or *rikiden no yakara*, usually owned this implement.[11] They employed the ox-drawn plow both on rice fields, where it was especially effective in returning abandoned paddies to a farmable state, and a growing acreage in dry tillage.

What makes Kōno's thesis especially attractive is the timing of the invention. According to the population figures calculated earlier, the middle Heian epoch seems to have been a time of some depopulation, meaning that there would have been a shortage of human labor power and lots of acreage for grazing animals. The development of the new harnessed plows pulled by oxen came about precisely, we might argue, to offset the labor shortfall and take advantage of wide-open spaces. These implements, of course, may have had their origins in an era of population loss, but when demographic recovery commenced after 1050, the same tools were available to create the additional fields later organized and taxed in the *shōen-kokugaryō* system. As Morris and others have argued, the ox-drawn plow began to assume its role in Japanese farming in the middle and later Heian period, but the demographic and economic conditions aiding its adoption were similar to those in depopulated fourteenth- and fifteenth-century Western Europe.[12]

Late Heian Agriculture

In 1967 Toda Yoshimi proposed the notion that the last century or so of the Heian period was an "age of widespread land clearance" *(dai kaikon jidai)*, and this idea spread almost without opposition in Japanese academe in the 1970s and 1980s.[13] As a paradigm drawn from European history, it was based upon two premises. First, as noted in the discussion of famine, the climate during the middle and late Heian period was assumed to have been unusually warm.[14] This weather would have allowed rice cultivation to spread into new regions, particularly northeastern Honshu, where, for example, the Fujiwara founded a rich kingdom at Hiraizumi. Second, the era 1050–1200 saw the establishment of the *shōen-kokugaryō* system, with many new estates being formed. Clearly, it seemed, farmers had to clear new land to support the rise of these innovative tenurial arrangements.

This interpretation still has supporters today. As more historians writing in the 1990s have addressed such topics as climate, famine and epidemics, and agrarian technology and land use, however, enthusiasm for the concept has waned considerably.[15] This section will list prominent proponents of this interpretation and critique their data and views, discuss the current status of the idea, and conclude with a brief summary of evidence on per-unit rice yields and the small improvements in the agrarian regime that did take place during the late Heian era.

Kimura Shigemitsu has been perhaps the most forceful advocate concerning the "age of widespread land clearance" purportedly occurring between 1050 and 1200.[16] As Kimura himself admits in the essay in which he developed this hypothesis, however, the "age of widespread land clearance" did not expand the arable over previous totals; farmers merely redeveloped fields that had fallen out of cultivation from earlier eras. When reviewers of his book pointed out the impropriety of applying the medieval European term to late Heian redevelopment, Kimura merely retorted that most fields were recleared from previous times.[17] A final blow to Kimura's reasoning came when one of his major examples, the creation of rice fields in Harima by Hata Tametatsu in 1079, turned out to have been based on forged and back-dated documents.[18]

In Kimura's view, dry fields comprised a large percentage of arable created in the late eleventh and early twelfth century. While wholeheartedly endorsing his emphasis on dry cropping, most critics have argued that he carried his argument too far by suggesting that once opened, dry fields remained continuously productive even as the acreage of wet-rice paddies annually expanded and contracted.[19] As Kimura states, dry fields did not even require surveying by the provincial headquarters until the second half of the eleventh century—possibly later.[20] The proposed reason for this official neglect was that government bureaucrats did not think the meager yields merited notice or taxation until that time.

Mizuno Shōji has been another supporter of the late Heian era as a time of great land clearance.[21] Yet his examples are less than convincing: In Ise and Yamato, almost all conversion of wilds into fields measured less than a single *chō* and much of the land was for housing *(kaito)*. Along the eastern shore of Lake Biwa, excavations indicate that human occupation plummeted in the tenth century, only to begin recovery in the twelfth century, and the field pattern *(jōri sei)* there did not take shape until after that time. In the case of Ōyama Estate in Tanba, as much as 50 percent of rice fields went uncultivated in three sections of the farm in the early twelfth century; in Mizuno's words, cropping in Ōyama was still "unstable."

To be sure, at one time scholars believed that a "stabilization" of rice cultivation took place in the late eleventh and twelfth centuries, an epoch that coincided with Toda's and others' "age of widespread land clearance." Inagaki Yasuhiko, who cited the case of Kohigashi Estate in Yamato (wherein the amount of abandoned land decreased by 10 *chō* between 1046 and 1108), was the chief proponent of the twelfth-century stabilization.[22] When Inagaki presented his case in 1975, he received immediate criticism from Nagahara Keiji, who pointed to high rates of land abandonment in estates of the twelfth, thirteenth, and fourteenth centuries. Inagaki tried to rebut Nagahara's evidence by asserting that all Nagahara's cases came from the hinterlands and not the advanced Kinai, but recently a tabulation of Kamakura-era estates, several of which were located in the capital region, has shown uncultivated fields bulking as large as 80 percent of the total.[23] Inagaki's thesis does not stand up to the scrutiny of later land records.

Kuroda Hideo is a more cautious, one-time advocate of the "age of widespread land clearance." While accepting this concept in the abstract, Kuroda has noted the following limitations. First, much land clearance was really the redevelopment of previously farmed areas; several special terms arose to denote these gone-to-waste fields, such as "pig-and-deer preserves" (*ishika no tateba*). Second, cultivators abandoned more than 50 percent of the arable in Sanuki during one stretch in the 1100s. Third, in contrast to Kimura, Kuroda asserts that there were two types of dry fields: those in constant cultivation and those not. Peasants frequently switched back and forth from dry to wet-rice cropping as the annual amount of rainfall varied. Fourth, the earliest case of paddy double-cropping, previously posited for Ise in 1118, seems to have taken place accidentally for one year only and the land was likely not resown the next winter, thus casting doubt on how systematic and widespread the practice was in the late Heian epoch. Kuroda also entertains strong suspicions about other instances of dry-field double-cropping suggested by Kimura for the eleventh and early twelfth centuries.[24]

Minegishi Sumio has analyzed another piece of evidence from archaeology.[25] In Gunma Prefecture in the 1970s, excavators uncovered a 12-kilometer-long irrigation ditch (*onnabori*) dating to the ancient period. Archaeologists removed volcanic ash from the top layer of the site, suggesting that the giant waterway had ceased functioning in the early twelfth century, when an eruption of Mt. Asama littered the Kanto with ash. Many fields undoubtedly went out of cultivation, only to be slowly brought back to a productive status as part of the "age of widespread land clearance." According to evidence presented by Harada Nobuo in his magisterial study of agriculture and settlement in eastern Honshu, "the age of widespread land clearance" never reached most of that area in the Heian era.[26]

Finally, recent research on Heian climate has led to greater emphasis on the problems arising from a decidedly warmer climate. To be sure, rice cultivation may have become possible on some alluvial plains where it had previously been too damp, and some farmers in cold eastern Honshu may well have been able to raise wet-rice for the first time. Nishiyachi Seibi, however, has argued that the higher mean temperatures would have induced drought in central and western Japan, hindered the propagation of dry crops such as wheat, led to more blight and insect infestations, and given rise to conditions conducive to the spread of malaria.[27]

Currently, Japanese scholars are divided between historians such as Nishiyachi and Iinuma Kenji, who stress harsh climate, famine, and epidemics leading to chronic agrarian crises, and geographers like Takahashi Manabu, who detect a greater trend toward the conversion of certain lands on the alluvial plains into productive fields.[28] Yet not all geographers agree with Takahashi. For instance, Kinda Akihiro has continued his path-breaking studies on the ancient agricultural landscape, shaped by the checkerboard pattern known as the *jōri sei*.[29] Once scholars believed that aerial photography revealed the antiquity of this field arrangement.[30] Now historical geographers rely upon ancient maps and documents as well as archaeological reports, which, Kinda believes, show a constant reworking of the land. He argues for three separate grid arrangements before 1150: one for the Nara allotment system from 690 to 900; a second functioning when the provincial headquarters held sway from 900 to 1050; and a third associated with the formation of the *shōen-kokugaryō* institution during the late Heian era. Although he envisions some advances by then, Kinda emphasizes that even under the *shōen-kokugaryō* system the grid was irregular, with individual blocs containing a mixture of productive rice paddies, abandoned fields, dry tillage, and unimproved land.

In sum, the tide seems to run against advocates of the "age of widespread land clearance." In particular, two facts presented in this essay help place this notion in its proper context. Archaeologists have shown that the eleventh century was a time of general land abandonment throughout the archipelago.[31] While the causes of this phenomenon remain poorly understood, it means that in effect the land clearance that served as the basis for the *shōen-kokugaryō* system between 1050 and 1200 was a mere reopening of once productive fields. Also, if the figures for total rice acreage in the mid-tenth century *Wamyō shō* (862,000 *chō*) and the mid-twelfth century *Shūgai shō* (956,000 *chō*) are credible, Japan's overall area of land under cultivation, or at least its rice paddies, expanded only 9.8 percent during the last half of the Heian period. This increase was likely responsible for the modest recovery in population by 1150.

Not only did productive fields grow only marginally between 950 and 1150, yields improved almost imperceptibly, according to Ishii Susumu.[32] In the best example to date, Ishii analyzed Ōba Estate, where figures are available for both yield in rice and area under cultivation. According to the record, Ōba contained 95 *chō*, which surrendered a harvest of 47,750 sheaves of rice in 1144. Simple division suggests that 1 *chō* produced about 502 sheaves that year, just barely above the amount for good rice paddies (*jōden*) 450 years earlier. To be sure, we have no way of knowing whether 1144 was a bountiful year or not or how estate officials graded the lands at Ōba, but according to Ishii this figure is representative of per-unit rice yields in the late Heian period. In other words, there was little growth over the Nara and Heian eras. With a nearly inelastic food supply, it is small wonder that population remained essentially static over that time.

To be sure, a few advances in late Heian agriculture may have augmented the food supply a bit. Most scholars, including both Kuroda and Kimura, assert that dry cropping of grains such as wheat, buckwheat, soybeans, millet, and barley became both somewhat more common and productive after about 1050.[33] Moreover, peasants made more intensive use of some land, converting it from a dry field to irrigated rice paddy. Kuroda also points to the initiation of several reclamation projects (shiotsutsumi), which rescued productive soils from the encroaching sea.[34] And, as Furushima Toshio and later Dana Morris have described, it is likely that more peasants came to possess iron spades, hoes, and sickles, employed in greater numbers for the more sophisticated type of rice cultivation requiring seedling transplantation.[35] A final technological advance was further diffusion of the plow and draft animals. Around 950, wealthy cultivators, known as tato or rikiden no yakara, were the only ones who could afford this technology, but as the population recovered a bit between 1050 and 1150, this implement spread to more households. Peasants employed the ox-drawn plow both on rice fields, where it was especially effective in returning abandoned paddies to a farmable state, and in increasing the number of dry fields.

In my view, documents and archaeological data stress the fundamental continuity between Nara and Heian rural life, with perhaps some marginal improvements in the latter epoch.[36] The advances, including more productive dry cropping, further diffusion of iron tools, and wider employment of the ox-drawn plow, were just beginning to make themselves felt by 1150. Productivity grew little and the rice acreage needed to support an individual was only slightly less than in 950 or even 750.

Settlement Patterns and Migration

As late as the 1960s, scholars such as Iyanaga Teizō asserted that ancient peasants' dwellings were huddled together in clustered settlements.[37] Since the 1970s and the research of the microgeographer Kinda Akihiro, most scholars have discarded Iyanaga's thesis in favor of the idea that ancient Japanese peasant dwellings formed isolated homesteads, small hamlets, or larger dispersed settlements.[38] Recently, Gina Barnes, Kristina Troost, and Dana Morris have reinforced this view.[39] Kinda has also written an essay tracing the evolution of these scattered forms into the compact, moat-encircled villages of the sixteenth century.[40]

Moreover, settlement boundaries and population movements were fluid, even though the government forbade migration.[41] We can trace this proposition back to Yoshida Takashi's path-finding research of the 1970s, and recent study has merely reinforced this posture. There seems to have been a substantial number of people in rural Japan who shifted their residences regularly, whether to flee the tax collector or search for food and shelter. Thomas Keirstead in his study of medieval estates gave voice to the same opinion.[42] Japanese scholars have pointed out that mobile peasants were particularly useful as labor gangs for field development.[43]

The scattered nature of rural settlement and the frequency of migration are probably related to population change in complex and contradictory ways. Isolated villages could well have reduced the spread of epidemic disease but also slowed the painful process of raising the immunity levels of the archipelago's inhabitants. Continuous geographic mobility could have acted to provide a ready pool for land clearance, separate couples during the woman's child-bearing years, and encourage trade, spread infections, and facilitate tax evasion—to name but a few possibilities.[44] Given these ambiguities, we can only ponder their net effect on population trends.

The Labor Market and Industry

Like agriculture and settlement, this variable describes and feeds into ancient demography indirectly and in complex ways. Possible indications of a declining population include a rise in wages, a decline in construction, or an increase in building projects that take longer to complete or are never finished. For instance, changes in the labor system and the slowing of monumental building during the later eighth century may well have denoted a dearth of healthy workers. By the early 800s, the tripartite work system, based on paid/forced labor (koeki), "service adults" (shichō), and the local corvée (zōyō), was coming acropper, as major construction came to a halt.[45] Government regulations make such statements as "emergency conscriptions [of workers] are many, while corvée adults are few" and "people are few although deterioration [of government facilities] is increasingly widespread."

A brief look at temple construction in the early ninth century sustains this impression. Not only did the raising of immense capitals cease at Heian in 819, but the main centers of the Tendai and Shingon sects encountered problems as well. In the cases of Tōji and Saiji, located at the southern entrance to Heian, Yoshito Hakeda asserts that in 823 "nearly thirty years had elapsed since the removal of the capital, but the construction of the new temples in Kyoto proceeded slowly with frequent changes of director. The unfinished buildings at the entrance to the city must have been unsightly."[46] As Kūkai fell seriously ill in 831, "he wished to return to the construction project [at Mt. Kōya] which had been lagging for years."[47] In the case of Enryakuji, political friction with the older Nara sects also played a role, but the original plan as laid out by Saichō called for "a large complex of buildings, as was shown by his [Saichō's] proposals for nine and later sixteen halls. During his lifetime he was able to complete only one or two of these buildings."[48] It is not difficult to believe that manpower shortfalls loomed large in the tardiness of construction.

Little is known of the labor system of the ninth century. Takinami Sadako has argued that the 800s saw the virtual end to corvée and the substitution of hired laborers (tsuku no hitobito).[49] In some cases, commoners paid their dues in commodities, which bureaucrats then utilized to hire the requisite labor. As local notables, represented by the district magistrates, lost control over the labor supply, corvée was no longer possible and hiring workers became the rule. Laborers could rely upon receiving food, wages (15–16 coins per day), and transportation costs for a maximum stint of 30 days. While these conditions are about the same as those for laborers on Japan's great projects of the eighth century, the average daily wage in the mid- and late 700s was only about 10 coins, suggesting rising payments in the face of a labor shortfall.[50] Of course, inflation may also have played a role in the raises given to these workers. The substitution of hired labor for corvée is highly reminiscent of conditions in Western Europe after the Black Death decimated the work force in the late fourteenth and fifteenth centuries.

In the tenth and eleventh centuries, the labor system once again took a different name, the "extraordinary levy" (rinji zōyaku).[51] As Cornelius Kiley has noted, this tax was anything but extraordinary, essentially being a complex amalgam of the local products and corvée levies of the eighth century.[52] Few historical materials have survived to reveal the nature of this tax; it appears wealthy farmers who headed the myō (name fields) raised labor gangs, although officials treated each individual as a tax unit. Sources indicate that the government most frequently called to duty peasants and local notables residing in the Kinai; even they were desirous of and frequently obtained exemption from this levy.

Because the "extraordinary levy" included local products such as cloth and metals as well as labor, it is difficult to judge exactly how the work force changed in the tenth and eleventh centuries. Moreover, the era 900-1050 is the most poorly documented time in the Heian period. Ōtsu Tōru has argued that appropriate "custodial governors" (zuryō) supplying laborers on an ad hoc basis completed most of the building: They reconstructed the frequently burned out imperial residence (dairi), refurbished the great wall (*ōgaki*) surrounding the palace, and periodically replaced Ise shrine. Precisely which provinces bureaucrats would call to duty depended upon their financial standing and the willingness of local politicians to curry favor, although between 800 and 950 workers came solely from the Kinai due to its geographical proximity to the construction projects.

There are many indications of labor problems: Provincial governors frequently resisted levies and tried to shift their duty onto others. The court abolished the Repair Agency (*shūri shiki*) for Heian in the early 800s and did not reestablish it until around 900. The government did not refurbish the imperial residence between the original raising of Heian around 800 and 960, while they did not redo the great wall around the palace grounds until 1005. There is no record of Ise Shrine being rebuilt between 900 and 1050. As far as primary sources are concerned, labor in the ninth, tenth, and eleventh centuries seems to have been exacted in a most unsystematic way, mainly through rich custodial governors, aristocrats, and even the Investigators Office (*kebiishi chō*). The prominent role played by private donations of labor and goods is yet another parallel to Western Europe after 1351.[53]

While in general written sources are not very helpful for the era 900–1050, there are a few cases that hint at the conditions of labor and construction. Paul Groner has pointed out that when the structures on Mt. Hiei burned down in 966, rebuilding was "difficult," and laborers did not complete the thirty-one buildings destroyed in the inferno until 984.[54] Mikael Adolphson notes that in the late tenth century, a conflagration destroyed the central structures of Mt. Koya and reconstruction was so slow that the monks left in protest.[55] Yet again in 1016, Michinaga ordered the reconstruction of his Tsuchimikado Mansion, but despite his stated desire to witness completion within six months, it took more than two years, even with the aid of several eager custodial governors. In 1019, Michinaga commanded the raising of an Amida Hall to declare his faith in salvation by the Buddha. Even with the support of donations from wealthy courtiers and governors and the use of recycled foundation stones and tiles, workers did not finish the new temple soon to be known as Hosshōji until 1021. When it burned in 1058, no one rebuilt it.[56]

Beginning in the late eleventh century, the name of the labor impost changed once again, becoming known as "equal corvée by province" (*ik-koku heikin yaku*).[57] The intent was to expand and systematize this levy on an archipelago-wide basis, including both estate and provincial lands even in territories outside the Kinai, but for the period 1100–1150 the court seems to have delegated most of the administration to provincial governors. The only problem was that the fiscal resources of not only the court but also most provinces had declined to such an extent that the central government had to resort to the sale of office and court rank *(jōkō sei)* to raise sufficient funds. While it is difficult to envision a building boom, the attempted expansion and greater systemization may indicate a more energetic construction policy; such a pattern fits with the minor population recovery inferred for the era from around 1150.

Still, though, for those government projects for which data are available, the record of completion was poor. For example, between 1100 and 1150, workers built the imperial residence anew only once, and that in 1100.[58] In fact, the official palace became so run-down that the government used it only for the accession ceremony, and most emperors spent their time in temporary residences *(sato dairi)*. Later in 1142, a court annal noted in reference to the dams on the Kamo River that "recently work has stopped and there are no repairs." Concerning government office buildings, the chronicler lamented that "the provinces responsible for constructing the Eight Ministries exist in name only. The palaces and halls of previous emperors have all become grass. Oh, what a scar!"[59]

When great aristocrats wanted to dip into their own pockets to build, however, they were much more likely to be successful. A good example is the famous Byōdōin of Uji, started by Regent Fujiwara no Yorimichi in 1052 and basically completed by the end of the following year. Yet even in this case there were signs of a possible shortage of labor and resources, as the model for the Uji treasure was father Michinaga's Hōjōji, which purportedly contained nine statues of Amida, not one as at Uji. Personal preference and religious reasons, of course, may also explain the difference in scale.[60]

Overall, the historical record seems to indicate that there was a scarcity of labor and that construction projects through most of the ancient age proceeded slowly, if at all. Of course, one difficulty with this argument is that the problem may have lain in the lack of building materials, not labor. Yet scarcity of supply increased the labor requirements of construction, adding to its difficulty, given the inability of elites to generate enough wages to lure workmen to jobs. In sum, the evidence on this factor is slim but seems to support the contention that population shrank in the ninth and tenth centuries, only to rebound a bit by 1150.

Industry

Technological changes arising within individual industries may also be a significant indicator of population trends. In other words, are new technologies being applied to industry? If so, what kind? Most importantly, what implications do they have for employment and fluctuations in the supply of workers? Are more labor-saving devices coming into use? Did some industries experience decline? The following section will briefly examine six widely differing industries in an effort to answer some of these questions.

Consider, for example, iron-working.[61] While both archaeological and written sources are fragmentary and Japanese historians have been cautious in addressing technological issues and differ considerably in their reading of the evidence, some points are becoming clearer. Of course, Japan is iron-poor, and furnaces for the smelting of iron sand and ore did not appear in western Honshu until around 500 CE. The first type was a low, rectangular, "box-shaped" (hakogata) furnace, complete with blowpipes (tuyeres, haguchi) and bellows. This apparatus, which may have had its origins in South China or Southeast Asia, entered the islands through Kyushu and western Honshu.

As the smelting of iron spread to eastern Honshu and became nativized in the late eighth century, a simpler design evolved. Called the "half-submerged vertical shaft furnace" (han chika shiki tategata ro), this device quickly became popular over much of the archipelago. Unlike the first, however, it seems to have required neither tuyeres nor bellows, the fire being fanned by updrafting wind since the furnace itself was often located on a slope. Throughout the ninth, tenth, and perhaps as late as the eleventh century, such "vertical shaft" furnaces, although more primitive and less efficient than the "box-shaped" ones, successfully produced enough ferrous material to supply residents of the archipelago, especially in the formerly iron-deficient Kanto. What is most significant here is that the "vertical shaft" model required no persons to pump bellows: a labor-saving device in a time of demographic decline. In some cases these furnaces were so simple that they were abandoned after only a short time in use. In Fukuda Toyohiko's phrase, iron production was experiencing a "step backward."[62] The spread of iron and iron products took place over the early and mid-Heian eras through a technology that could operate in a labor-short economy.

Silk thread and cloth were products highly desired by the elite.[63] Their manufacture in Japan dates to about 500 CE, but the Nara court gave it a big boost by ordering silk-making, recruiting experts, importing technology, and consuming large quantities. Not only did silk manufacture increase and spread to the provinces, but for the first time the court introduced the technology of silk-reeling. These improvements turned out to be short-lived, however, as decline set in from the early Heian era. While no figures are available, sources state that both the amount and quality deteriorated until the twelfth century.[64] Damasks and brocades worn by Prince Genji and other civil aristocrats were either imported or produced by a few female weavers attached to a noble's house.

Transportation was another sector of the economy that experienced retrogression. Travel technology—boats, packhorses, wooden carts, and foot traffic—did remain essentially the same in the days of Lady Murasaki as in the Nara age. With the demise of Chinese-style institutions after 800, however, the government no longer built roads and the all-important system of post-stations suffered from both a lack of manpower and funds. Records suggest that the efficiency of transportation fell off markedly. For example, during the eighth century, a boat trip from Dazaifu to Nara required about 5–6 days; by the Heian era travel time had doubled to 12 days. Going overland from Mutsu to the capital in the 700s usually consumed 8 days, but by the mid-Heian era travel time was nearly 2 weeks. The leisurely journeys of Prince Genji's day were no accident.[65]

Salt production is a fourth example of industrial change in the face of new demographic and economic realities. Ever since the Jōmon age, inhabitants of the archipelago had manufactured salt by evaporating seawater. The earliest technology utilized earthenware pots in which laborers heated the seawater until they produced crystal salt. People of the Tomb era, however, added a new wrinkle: Not only did they substitute iron cauldrons for clay pots, but enterprising salt-makers began to hasten the process by which the salt became concentrated in water by draining the saline solution over seaweed. This process enabled the seaweed to extract some of the water from the solution, accelerating the formation of salt crystals in the residue. Much labor, however, was required to make the cauldrons; collect the seawater, seaweed, and firewood; and pour the ever-thickening solution continuously over the outstretched seaweed.[66]

Beginning in the late ninth century, however, a technological innovation began to impinge upon salt-making. Salt-makers constructed "salt-fields" (*shiohama*) on the shore to trap ocean waves, thereby allowing the sun to evaporate the water and converting the chore of salt-making into one of salt collection. Not only did the newer method require less labor and equipment, but it was faster and produced more salt. It is notable that these salt-fields became the favored method of production just as population declined, another technological adaptation to changed demographic conditions.[67]

The shift to labor-saving technologies is harder to recognize for the late eleventh and early twelfth centuries, but it is by no means absent. Perhaps the best case of adjustment for any era occurred in one of the most basic crafts: ceramics. By the eighth century, most people preferred Sue ware, a type of stoneware originally imported from the southern Korean peninsula. In addition, commoners widely preferred Haji earthenware and Tang porcelains were available for the aristocracy. During the eleventh and twelfth centuries, however, the ceramic industry showed unmistakable signs of change:

The volume and variety of dishes uncovered in excavation sites all over the archipelago decreased markedly. According to archaeologist Shiraishi Taichirō, these changes represent a "simplification and greater efficiency" in pot making, a transformation that fits perfectly with the shortage of both firewood and labor.[68]

Lacquerware was another sector where innovation was the watchword in the early twelfth century.[69] During the eighth century, state-run offices turned out a small quantity of lacquered plates and saucers using a method known as *urushi shitaji*. From about 1100, however, a new technique *(shibu shitaji)* overtook the industry, leading to the mass production of a variety of cheap saucers and small plates brushed with persimmon juice *(shibu)* instead of the more expensive and difficult-to-work lacquer. Not only was the new process simpler and less time-consuming, it reached a broader class of consumers.[70]

Finally, the overall trend in craft organization for the late Heian era is also noteworthy.[71] From the late eleventh century the medieval guild *(za)* first entered the historical record. Kozo Yamamura has already treated these groups in some detail; he described their creation as enhancing specialization while at the same time limiting competition. Both phenomena are consistent with a somewhat larger population and a developing trade and industrial sector, such as existed in the late eleventh and first half of the twelfth century.

The industries discussed above are not all-inclusive; undoubtedly future research will make the picture clearer. At least in the case of these six crafts, however, technological evolution seems to correspond well to the demographic realities laid out in this essay. Other cases—such as the widespread employment of the crossbow in the ninth century to compensate for the demise of massive conscripted forces—seem to bolster the argument made here. In any event, the foregoing picture of industrial development corresponds rather well to the demographic curve adduced earlier.

TRADE AND URBANIZATION

Mercantile activity is yet another indirect variable relating to population in diverse ways. In general, vigorous commercial development may support and supplement growth, as when surplus grain becomes available during a local famine or peasants have the opportunity to purchase better tools or fertilizers. One must be careful with this factor, however, as societies experiencing population decline or stasis may also possess a lively commercial sector.

Unfortunately, trade has been a neglected aspect of the ancient economy in English. Close examination of the evidence for the eighth and ninth centuries indicates that commerce was an important, if secondary, means for provisioning the urban populace in Nara and Heian.[72] In fact, over the course of the late eighth and ninth centuries, trade *(kōeki)* became a crucial aspect of government finance; as central government coffers became empty, the court prevailed upon provincial governors to exchange their reserves of loan rice with artisans for aristocratic necessities. The heyday of this policy was about 770–850; the frittering away of fiscal reserves continued into the tenth century, when the policy was gradually replaced by the "extraordinary tax" described above.

Moreover, the court minted copper cash, beginning in 708 and ceasing in 958. As Japanese historians and archaeologists have shown, a financially strapped central government continually debased the coinage in the ninth and tenth centuries as it tried to enhance its profit from the mint. By the late tenth century, the court was complaining frequently about the failure of the populace to use its coins. In 984 a record stated that "the world has never avoided the use of cash more than it does now"; in 987 an order was delivered to the Investigators to have "people of all ranks employ coins in their transactions."[73] Rice became the chief unit of accounting, and barter must have been prevalent.

The brief outline presented above suggests an economy in which trade eventually occupied a smaller niche and demonetization occurred. As implied above, the general assumption in economics is that an increase in trade and growing monetization indicate greater social specialization, often due to population growth. Trends in the opposite direction may not necessarily prove economic retrogression and population decline, but they may be suggestive. Furthermore, trade does not have to cease when the population declines, even precipitously; commerce grew in late medieval Europe even as the plague was reducing the number of inhabitants by as much as a third. The same was also true of early modern Japan beginning around 1720, when population stabilized but commerce boomed. Overall, however, demonetization and a slowing of exchange velocity until the late Heian era fits the population curve detailed above.

From the mid-eleventh century, however, conditions slowly improved, once again in line with the modest population recovery inferred previously. In northern Kyushu, Sung captains in command of sizable junks commenced calling by about 1000; by the late eleventh and early twelfth centuries, these Chinese merchants were providing attractive, well-made goods, and more importantly cash to local Japanese traders.[74] Sung commerce was so vigorous that courtiers in Kyoto were unable to manage it effectively; Sung merchants married Kyushu women and adopted Japanese surnames. In 1151, when two samurai led an attack on the northern Kyushu ports of Hakata and Hakozaki, fleeing Chinese merchants numbered more than 1,600 families.[75]

Stimulated by Sung commercial dynamism, domestic trade rebounded. Producer-merchants "traveled to more and more distant provinces" from the 1050s, and a metropolitan Kyoto exchange center, probably similar to the one created in the eighth century for Nara, evolved and commercial markets and rich traders became more common at about the same time.[76] Merchants formed the first medieval guild in 1092, and they created more in the next decades of the Heian era. Following Sasaki Gin'ya and Kozo Yamamura, we may stipulate that even though estates and provincial lands provided the lion's share of consumer goods, trade "increased steadily" beginning in 1050, a phenomenon consistent with the recovery of the population hypothesized earlier.[77]

Cities

Fluctuation in the number and size of cities corresponds closely to the transformation of commerce. In the eighth century, there were three major cities: Nara, its port and co-capital Naniwa, and Dazaifu. While it is impossible to know for certain the population of these centers, Nara was home to 70,000–100,000 residents, with Naniwa and Dazaifu adding perhaps another 50,000. Furthermore, every one of the sixty-odd provinces had its own capital *(kokufu)*, some of which housed as many as 600 officials and other occupants. Adding about 1,000 persons per *kokufu*, which may well be a conservative estimate, the total urban population of eighth-century Japan was perhaps about 200,000.[78]

Over the period of the ninth, tenth, and eleventh centuries, the size of the archipelago's urban population likely diminished. William McCullough has calculated the population of Heian at around 100,000, but of course Nara shrank drastically after 784.[79] At the end of eighth century, Naniwa was inundated by a flood of the Yamato River, and its abolition as a secondary capital in 784 undoubtedly also promoted a steep demise. Dazaifu continued to function throughout the Heian era, but two points suggest decline during the tenth and early eleventh centuries: First, in the latter half of the 800s, the court's official trade with the continent fell off as governmental relations were terminated with the failing Tang and Silla dynasties; and second, in 941 the pirate Fujiwara Sumitomo burned the port. An attack in 1019 by Jurchen nomads also probably had deleterious effects.[80] Finally, the size of many provincial capitals dwindled, and they were later removed to other locations in the early and mid-Heian era.[81] This shrinkage and disappearance of towns and cities between 800 and 1050 is another sign of an overall demographic drop-off during that epoch.

As in the case of commerce, the last century of the Heian period saw a rebound in the number and size of cities. While the total figure for Kyoto inhabitants may have remained about the same, Dazaifu gained a new lease on life with the Sung trade: Port facilities sprang up and merchants and their families congregated there.[82] The center of the new city, however, moved to Hakata, which probably reached a population of several thousand by 1150. Other small centers, including Ōtsu, Kizu, Toba, Yodo, Hyōgo, and Sakamoto near Kyoto; Wakasa and Yamazaki in western Honshu; and Hiraizumi in northeastern Honshu, also began to come to prominence in the late eleventh and early twelfth centuries.[83] The gradual reurbanization of the last one hundred years of the Heian period reflects and supports the demographic trend posited above, although it is impossible to determine whether Japan's urban dwellers in 1150 outnumbered those of 730. The estimate used above when calculating the archipelago-wide population for 1150 was 200,000, but given the greater number of towns and the volume of trade, it may have been even more substantial.

KINSHIP, MARRIAGE, AND THE FAMILY

These variables probably have the largest influence on fertility and infant mortality, and while Japanese scholars have evinced a great interest in all three of these topics, there are at least two major problems. First, the scanty nature of the sources restricts study of the overwhelming majority that comprised the commoner class. This is particularly true for the early and middle Heian periods. Second, scholars have directed almost none of the research from a demographic perspective—that is, drawing conclusions about the birth rate or percentage of children surviving infancy. Even basic questions must go begging: What was the average size of the peasant family upon completion? What was the usual interval between offspring? Neither archaeology nor even the census registers, which record two types of "households" (gōko and bōko) averaging 10–30 members, are of any help for these questions.[84]

The only quantitative answers available come from the household registers of the early eighth century; fertility was extraordinarily high (about 45–50 per 1,000 per year) and infant mortality was at least 50 percent to age 5.[85] (See Table 3.) These conclusions are not especially surprising because demographers generally assume that in premodern societies, especially those occurring as long ago as Nara and Heian Japan, women gave birth about as often as physically possible and many babies died in infancy. It is generally believed that there were few means of contraception, and in any event large families were viewed positively for several reasons. Given the size and origin of the samples, however, we are justified in doubting whether birth rates ever achieved and maintained such a lofty height. In particular, the registers show a large percentage of childless women, a fact flatly contradicting the inferred high fertility.

Because quantitative data are unavailable after the early eighth century, and suspicions may be entertained about even that information, we are forced to rely almost exclusively on descriptive accounts of kinship, marriage, and the family. This section will attempt to glean from these discussions facts relevant to the fertility and infant mortality of the general populace, concluding with a summary of these crucial subjects.

Regarding kinship, a majority of Japanese historians concur in the opinion that in the ancient age it was bilateral.[86] This means that a family's lineage could be traced through either the father's or mother's line; not only are the law codes clear on this point, but archaeological evidence, as well as the frequent reference to dual surnames in the household registers, seems to bolster the case for the population at-large.[87] As Robin Fox, a noted anthropologist, has asserted, bilateral relations make for high "mobility and an easy distribution of the population over farming units."[88] Under this system of kinship, it appears as though there would have been less likelihood of overcrowding, and families would have had more outlets for numerous offspring, encouraging a high birth rate.

In a related point, commoner families with property to pass down to heirs—given the fluidity and mobility of ancient Japanese society there may not have been too many—practiced partible inheritance. The Household Statutes (ko-ryō) of the Yōrō Code gave a small preference to the male heir, but according to a commentary on the Taihō Code, this rule applied only to the wealthy; for the rest of the populace, property was to be "divided equally."[89] This guideline was enforced for daughters as well as sons. Such a custom suggests that population density was low, there being little or no pressure on available resources, such as land.[90] As was true for the late Tokugawa era or Western Europe on the eve of the Black Death, premodern families usually turned to unigeniture only when farmland was in short supply. The wide-open spaces of ancient Japan probably encouraged families to have as many children as possible.

The nature of Nara and Heian marriage is also consistent with high fertility. To elaborate, we note that even as late as the eighth century, duolocal residence was the rule, with the wife naming and raising the children and maintaining considerable property rights and economic power.[91] Moreover, *The Chronicles of Japan* and other anthropological data indicate that prospective husbands provided their mates-to-be with property (called "bridewealth" or "brideprice") to secure the nonexclusive right to have children with her.[92] With the arrival of the Heian period, however, the form of marriage changed somewhat. Duolocal residence essentially ended and the husband usually took to living with his wife and her relatives. This type of marriage arrangement was termed "take in the husband" (mukotori kon). Takamure Itsue, a pioneering researcher in this field, argued that the pattern of marriage she had observed—that is, a slow transition from duolocal to uxorilocal relations between 700 and 1150—held true not just for the tiny elite of civil aristocrats, but for the commoner population as well.[93]

The critical point is that there were no set ceremonies defining either the start or termination of sexual relations for any of these types of marriage. As poetry from Man'yōshū and other sources suggests, young men and women began pairing off at a young age, exchanging lyrics and nightly visits. Nothing really indicated that a man had "married" a woman or that their relationship was exclusive or life-long. If one tired of the other, the visits simply stopped or the husband left. Wives had as much right to terminate a "marriage" as did husbands.[94] Furthermore, ancient Japan possessed no restrictions against members of the same family "marrying," particularly when they had the same father but different mothers (and therefore may well have been raised in separate residences). Finally, another custom allowed brothers to inherit their kin's widows, again probably boosting fertility.[95] This vague distinction between "married" and "unmarried" couples contradicted the law codes, which in high-sounding Chinese terminology required notice of marriage and divorce, but this facet was one of many where the Japanese practice was at odds with the Chinese. Japanese custom could well have led to frequent changes in partners and lots of pregnancies.[96]

Moreover, Takamure suggested a reason for the gradual conversion from duolocal to uxorilocal residence—a shortage of labor. In farm families, this lack of hands was especially true by the middle Heian period, exactly the time when figures derived above suggest a drop in archipelago-wide population. Although he approached the issue from a different angle, utilizing household registers, the doubtful character of which has already been noted, Dana Morris arrived at the same conclusion as Takamure: The relatively large size of Heian peasant families was a device to secure labor.[97]

In fact, kinship, marriage, and the shortage of labor were intertwined and help to suggest why women enjoyed such high status throughout the ancient period. First, in an age when there were no paternity tests, the only way to determine to whom a child belonged was through the mother, especially in a society where women often took on different partners. Second, among the wealthier classes, such as aristocrats and local notables, it was common for powerful men to practice polygamy, thus reducing the pool of potential mates for the less fortunate. Under such circumstances, women could command considerable power over their work, possessions, residences, slaves, and children. This link between a shortage of labor, bilateral kinship, and bridewealth was particularly widespread among the peoples of Southeast Asia.[98]

Three final points are important in any consideration of birth rates and infant mortality. First, the frequent epidemics and famines probably operated to lower fertility over long periods. With one crisis or another coming about every other year, the populace may have been hard-pressed to achieve the maximum possible birth rate. Second, as Kōchi Shōsuke pointed out more than twenty years ago, the legislation of a minimum age to receive a land grant (six years) probably arose because of the high rate of infant mortality.[99] Even as late as the medieval era, children were not expected to live beyond age seven. Third, eighth- and ninth-century Japanese society was comprised of about 5–10 percent slaves (*nuhi*), whose families could be broken up by sale, a condition probably lowering fertility for a significant portion of the populace.[100]

In sum, available evidence on kinship, marriage, and the family is slender and scholars can read it in many different ways. We might argue that it is only marginally helpful in divining birth and infant mortality rates, which are so crucial to any understanding of the ancient demographic regime. Insofar as we can believe this data, however, it would appear to suggest that both of these critical demographic indicators were high. But the constant recurrence of pestilence and famine often lowered fertility while increasing mortality for infants. Such a conclusion need not be out-of-line with the general population curve adduced in this book.

Commoner Physical Well-Being

In *Everyday Things in Premodern Japan,* Susan Hanley raised the critical but often unexamined question of peoples' general physical well-being during the Tokugawa era. As Hanley points out, this factor, which includes elements such as housing, clothing, diet, and sanitation, is often difficult to assess. The overall quality of material well-being, however, is yet another indirect measure affecting fertility and mortality. Despite even greater handicaps inherent in investigating this topic a thousand years earlier, we should include a brief consideration of commoner material well-being over the era 700–1150 in any evaluation of ancient demography.

To describe housing first, the pit dwelling (*tateana jūkyo*) remained the basic unit for the general populace over the Nara and Heian eras.[101] Standing 3–4 meters to a side, these huts had been the typical residence for the overwhelming majority since the Jōmon era. By 700 it usually had four posts planted in the ground upon which residents built a wooden frame; the entire structure was then covered with grasses. In most of the archipelago, the earthen floor was set below ground level, and occupants probably spread straw or dried leaves for bedding. Food was cooked over an open fire *(ro)* until the fifth century; from that time boiler *(kamado)* technology entered the archipelago via southern Korea and gradually spread until it was fairly common in western Japan by 700.[102]

Beginning in the seventh century in the central Kinai and continuing into the mid-Heian period in central Honshu, a slow change began to overtake housing: Lowered floors disappeared and people carried out their daily lives at ground level.[103] In a few cases, larger houses with floorboards have been detected, but these were restricted to a small elite of wealthy local notables. Expanded wooden homes complete with floorboards first appeared in the Kinai but did not reach the Tohoku until the Muromachi age.[104] For the general peasantry, the basic pattern was still to eat and sleep on pounded earth. In fact, in the Kanto, where the pit dwelling remained the predominant structure, it shrunk in size and became poorer in internal facilities as the Heian period advanced.[105] Overall, the dwelling that served as home to the general populace of the Nara and Heian eras must have been cramped, drafty, and prone to fire, a living structure consistent with people struggling on the edge of subsistence.

Clothing repeats the same theme. For the period 700–1150, the ordinary apparel for peasants was made from ramie *(karamushi)*, a variety of nettle, or hemp *(taima, mafu)*. Hemp was native to Japan from the Jōmon age, and Yayoi peasants planted it. They produced thread by stripping the outer skin of the stalk then drying and twisting the best fibers. According to Nagahara Keiji, the garment so woven not only consumed an inordinate amount of the family's labor but was cold and stiff, affording little protection or comfort.[106] Footwear was typically made of straw or perhaps not even worn at all. Ancient clothing seems to have provided little protection from the natural elements.

Diet and nutrition for commoners are crucial variables about which there is much controversy. There is even disagreement as to the main ingredients in the average person's diet. Scholars usually posit that peasants consumed rice, sometimes in gruel form; this position is supported by numerous orders for provisions for unskilled workers, which always prominently included brown rice.[107] Yet it is also asserted that peasants ate wheat and barley, particularly during famines. Other frequently mentioned items are salt, seaweed, bean paste, vinegar, melons, a wide variety of vegetables, and usually rice wine. Many people undoubtedly supplemented their diets with local fish and game. Chestnuts, mushrooms, and other fare gathered from forests must have been important.

Two facts raise doubts about this relatively optimistic view. First, the frequent famines left a large percentage of the population in a state of chronic or recurrent malnutrition, subject to what has become known as the "spring hungers." Second, lower-ranking bureaucrats probably ate better than the general populace, but even those lucky enough to land a government job did not eat well and saw their diet deteriorate over the eighth and ninth centuries.[108]

Because there is great uncertainty about what and how much the average commoner ate, there is no hope of computing average daily caloric intake. One indicator that may be useful is height, with men averaging 5 feet 3 inches and women under 5 feet in the late Yayoi period. Moreover, suits of armor uncovered from the Tomb period are tiny. By contrast, after World War II, when the Japanese diet improved sharply, there was a stunning increase in average height. These points seem to suggest that the ancient diet was "adequate" but minimally so, just enough to continue to reproduce the species.

Sanitation is a final critical element in everyday life. Susan Hanley has described the effective hygiene in early modern Japanese cities, due in part to the lucrative market in night soil for application as fertilizer.[109] In the ancient epoch, however, no such custom existed, and laws and diaries make Kyoto seem like a sewer in which people lived. Takahashi Masaaki has studied this problem; based upon Kyoto's population, he has estimated that urbanites produced 18,250 kiloliters of waste annually. The city had more than 370 bridges spanning about 700 kilometers of roadside ditches, which contained the microbe-laden garbage from the urban complex.[110] Laws specified that these ditches, in some sense the lifelines of the city, should be cleaned out periodically, but Takahashi has described the unsanitary conditions of the great city in which several streets and by-ways were given names such as "excrement alley" (kuso kōji).[111] Moreover, the corpses of beggars, abandoned children, and ailing servants often lay in the streets and large numbers of dead during epidemics and famines.[112] Like most premodern cities, Kyoto was an unhygenic cesspool of bacteria.

The issue of public health can be of great demographic consequence, but more research is needed to fill out the picture for ancient Japan. This brief description of material conditions—housing, clothing, diet, and sanitation—seems to lend credence both to the deadly role of microbes and the population trend inferred above.

NOTES

1. Yoshida Takashi, "Ritsuryō sei to sonraku," in *Iwanami kōza Nihon rekishi* 3 *Kodai* 3 (Iwanami shoten, 1976), 158, 170–71. For the best overviews of the seasonal cultivation cycle, see Furushima Toshio, *Furushima Toshio chosaku shū* 6 *Nihon nōgyō gijutsu shi* (Tokyo daigaku shuppan kai, 1975), 157–69; Toda Yoshimi, "Nōgyō rōdō to sonraku," in *Chūsei shakai no seiritsu to tenkai* (Yoshikawa kōbunkan, 1976), 309–31.

In particular, archaeologists and environmental historians have discovered several examples of the cyclical clearance and abandonment of fields and settlements. For example, see Miyataki Kōji, "'Saga-chō' ki ni okeru tōgoku shūraku no saikentō," *Kodai bunka* 54 (November 2002): 19–26; Terauchi Takao, "Kōshoku jōri iseki Yashiro iseki gun ni miru saigai to kaihatsu," *Kokuritsu reikishi minzoku hakubutsukan kenkyū hōkoku* 96 (March 2002): 23–52.

2. Tsude Hiroshi, *Nihon nōkō shakai no seiritsu katei* (Iwanami shoten, 1989), 85–93, 490–91.

3. Harashima Reiji, "Hasseiki no inasaku ni kansuru ni san no mondai," *Rekishi hyōron* 148 (December 1962): 29–31. Notably, all percentages dated from after the smallpox epidemic of 735–37.

4. Cornelius Kiley, "Provincial Administration and Land Tenure in Early Heian," in Donald H. Shively and William McCullough, eds., *The Cambridge History of Japan* (Cambridge: Cambridge University Press, 1999), 2:283–326; quotations come from pp. 305 and 325. It should be noted that the thrust of my argument differs somewhat from Kiley's. Also see Sakamoto Shōzō, *Nihon ōchō kokka taisei ron* (Tokyo daigaku shuppan kai, 1972), 140–57.

5. Despite the plentiful evidence on land abandonment in the ninth and tenth centuries, there is a prominent neo-Marxist argument implying a purported increase in population density (or more precisely "worker-to-arable ratio") deduced from changes in the tax system, most specifically rice loans. See Sonoda Kōyū, "Suiko: Tenpyō kara Engi made," in *Ritsuryō kokka no kiso kōzō* (Yoshikawa kōbunkan, 1960), 397–466; in English, see Dana Morris, "Land and Society," in Shively and McCullough, eds., *The Cambridge History of Japan*, 2:200–215. In the early 1960s, Sonoda traced the evolution of the system of provincial rice loans from a head tax to a land tax over the epoch 730–925. In the eighth century, provincial officials loaned peasants rice sheaves and then at harvest time collected the principal along with 30–50 percent interest; by the early 900s, loans were no longer made; each cultivator in theory was liable nonetheless for a set tribute tax that represented the old 30–50 percent interest. Some scholars have taken this change to have been a crucial development, variously signifying (1) an expansion of grain receipts, behind which lay productivity growth; and (2) an increase in the worker-to-arable ratio. As population soared, the government altered the basis of its revenue system from a more common and less valuable resource (persons/labor) to a rarer and richer commodity (fields).

While it is true that by the late tenth century the system of rice loans had become a land tax, there are several problems with Sonoda's analysis; see Hayakawa Shōhachi, "Ritsuryō zaisei no kōzō to sono henshitsu," in Iyanaga Teizō, ed., *Nihon keizai shi taikei* 1 *Kodai* (Tokyo daigaku shuppan kai, 1965), 276–80. As Sakamoto Shōzō (*Ōchō kokka taisei*, 181–88; *Nihon no rekishi* 6 *Sekkan jidai* [Shōgakkan, 1974], 140–42) and Nishiyachi Seibi ("Kajishi to suiko," *Iwanami kōza Nihon tsūshi* 7 *Chūsei* 1 [Iwanami shoten, 1993], 313–28; "Chūsei seiritsu ki ni okeru kajishi no seikaku,"

CHAPTER 3

Nihon shi kenkyū 275 [July 1985]: 1–25) have argued, the basic components of the
"new" late tenth-century land tax—the old Taihō grain levy *(denso)* along with the
interest portion of the loan system and some other minor imposts—all had their
roots in the 700s. In essence, the basic rate of taxation in rice remained the same or
even less, all the way from the eighth into the early twelfth century. As there was no
rise in land tax rates, we cannot use the statistic to conclude that a significant jump in
productivity per unit occurred. Moreover, these works also point out that abandoned
land was often included among productive fields when taxes were levied, rendering
the equation of a change in taxation with a rise in the worker-to-arable even less
tenable.

The foundation for much of the current knowledge of the tenth-century tax system is the famous Protest from the District Magistrates and People of Owari, dated
to 988 (*Kodai seiji shakai shisō*, 253–68; *Heian ibun*, edited by Takeuchi Rizō [Tokyo
dō, 1965], 2:473–85). While Japanese research is rich, the most succinct and accurate
analysis remains one written by Iyanaga Teizō (*Zusetsu Nihon no rekishi 5 kizoku to
bushi* [Iwanami shoten, 1980], 130–58) more than twenty years ago. On this point of
tax rate, see pp. 136–38. And as Iyanaga observed (pp.134–35), many "excessive"
taxes that Governor Fujiwara no Motonaga was accused of levying merely signaled
a return to levels that had prevailed in the eighth century. In some cases, his rate of
taxation was less than half the amount that had been common 250 years earlier. The
idea that taxes—and productivity—increased markedly between 700 and 1000 seems
even more doubtful after a careful reading of the Owari protest.

Finally, there are several difficulties with positing an increase in the worker-
to-arable ratio from these changes in the tax system. One oft-repeated assumption
by those who adhere to this position is that the revenues of the Taihō Code were
primarily labor levies because that was the scarcest commodity in 702. The Japanese scholar who advanced this idea, Murao Jirō, argued that essentially all *ritsuryō*
taxes could be converted into per capita days of labor, signifying the overwhelming
importance of that factor of production; see Murao Jirō, *Ritsuryō zaisei shi no kenkyū*
(Yoshikawa kōbunkan, 1961), 1–130; Kozo Yamamura, "The Decline of the *Ritsuryō*
System: Hypotheses on Economic and Institutional Change," *Journal of Japanese Studies* 1 (autumn 1974): 8.

As Hayakawa Shōhachi argued in his critical review of Murao's monograph,
however, the 3–5 percent grain tax *(denso)* was based on area of cultivation, and the
local products levy was paid in cloth or other commodities; neither had anything to
do with days of labor. Rather, it is better to think of the taxes collected by the Nara
court as falling into three categories: a light grain tax, local products levy, and the
corvée; see Hayakawa Shōhachi, "Hihyō to shōkai," *Shigaku zasshi* 71 (August 1962):
76–83. Finally, the two types of corvée—one lasting for ten days a year, the other
for as many as sixty days—were either usually collected in cloth or another good
or never enforced to the full legal limit. Drawing conclusions about the worker-to-
arable ratio based upon these legal ideals seems risky.

In sum, the view that the evolution of the provincial system of rice loans into
a land tax by the mid-tenth century necessarily connotes a concomitant rise in
the worker-to-arable ratio and the value of land is similarly doubtful. Rather, the
following interpretation seems at least as plausible as the one advanced by advocates
of agrarian and population growth. When population declined over the ninth and
tenth centuries, it became more difficult to locate peasants willing or able to take

interest-bearing loans. Furthermore, the central government was consuming the principal rapidly; soon there was no more rice to loan out of government warehouses. In place of making loans to individual peasants, government officials made wealthy farmers (*tato, rikiden no yakara*) responsible for what used be the interest on principal, based on the area of land that they farmed. This tax unit later came to be called a "name field," or *myō*.

From the point of view of the provincial headquarters, it was more straightforward and easier to tax a few rich farmers than to try to find each individual peasant. Assembling the requisite cultivators then became the problem of the wealthy, taxed farmer; if he failed, he would have to pay anyway. How did wealthy taxpayers gather willing cultivators? They doled out rice seed and food at more attractive rates than the provincial government had done before. In fact, this custom continued at least into the sixteenth century in a ritual known as *kannō* ("encourage agriculture").

In other words, the burden of making and collecting loans disappeared as the provincial governments sought to raise what revenues they could from wealthy residents. The withdrawal of officialdom from the details of taxation and increased reliance upon a few rich local growers fit well with what is known of middle Heian institutional and social history. Conditions in rural Japan in the tenth century were a good deal more complicated than a mere change in the unit of taxation from the individual to land might imply. In the circumstances as they truly existed, such an alteration in the tax unit more probably indicates a reform in the *means* of tax collection amidst population loss.

6. Furushima, *Furushima Toshio chosaku shū*, 143–44; Morris, "Land and Society," 2:186–89.

7. The sources for the plow are listed in Furushima, *Furushima Toshio chosaku shū*, 143–44. See *Konjaku monogatari shū*, edited by Yamada Takao et al. (Iwanami shoten, 1961), 3:443; *Utsubo monogatari* (Iwanami shoten, 1959–62), 1:339; *Shin sarugakki*, in *Kodai seiji shakai shisō*, edited by Takeuchi Rizō et al. (Iwanami shoten, 1979), 138; *Engi daizen shi shiki*, 878–79; *Shohon shūsei Wamyō ruijū shō: Honbun hen* (Kyoto: Rinsen shoten, 1968), 271, 722.

8. Kimura Shigemitsu, "Chūsei zenki no nōgyō seisanryoku to hatasaku," *Nihon shi kenkyū* 280 (December 1985): 65–67.

9. Thomas Smith, *The Agrarian Origins of Modern Japan* (Stanford: Stanford University Press, 1959), 25, 142. Smith concluded that plows and livestock played a relatively minor role in the development of Japanese agriculture; see also Tsude, *Nihon nōkō shakai no seiritsu katei*, 18, 284.

10. Kōno Michiaki, *Nihon nōkō gu shi no kisoteki kenkyū* (Izumi shoin, 1994), is an exhaustive study of the plow in Japan; see especially 280–97.

11. Ibid.; Kiley, "Provincial Administration and Land Tenure," 279–82, 313–14, 329–37.

12. Robert Gottfried, *The Black Death* (New York: The Free Press, 1983), 138.

13. Toda Yoshimi, *Nihon ryōshu sei seiritsu shi no kenkyū* (Iwanami shoten, 1967), 326–27. Scholars who spread the idea in the 1970s and 1980s include Kuroda Hideo, Kimura Shigemitsu, Mizuno Shōji, Inagaki Yasuhiko, and Minegishi Sumio, as listed below in notes 15, 16, 21, 22, and 25, respectively.

14. The initial and strongest proponent of this view is Yamamoto Takeo, "Rekishi no nagare ni sou Nihon to sono shūhen no kikō hensen," *Chigaku zasshi* 75 (March 1967): 119–41; *Kikō no kataru Nihon rekishi* (Soshiete bunko, 1976), 11–21. Toda endorsed

the idea in his *Shoki chūsei shakai shi no kenkyū*, 4. Ishii Susumu also endorsed it in *Nihon no chūsei 1 Chūsei no katachi* (Chūō kōron sha, 2002), 15–17. Also see Minegishi Sumio, *Chūsei no saigai senran no shakai shi* (Yoshikawa kōbunkan, 2001), 38–39; Isogai Fujio, *Chūsei no nōgyō to kikō* (Yoshikawa kōbunkan, 2002), 194–96.

15. See Gomi Fumihiko, "Chūseiteki tochi shoyū no tokushitsu to gaikan," and Nishiyachi Seibi and Iinuma Kenji, "Chūseiteki tochi shoyū no tokushitsu to kankyō," in Gomi Fumihiko and Watanabe Hisashi, eds., *Shin taikei Nihon shi 3 Tochi shoyū shi* (Yamakawa shuppan, 2002), 77–113.

Or consider the writings of Kuroda Hideo of the Historiographical Institute at Tokyo University: *Nihon chūsei kaihatsu shi no kenkyū* (Azekura shobō, 1984) and "Chūsei no kaihatsu to shizen," in *Ikki 4 Seikatsu bunka shisō* (Tokyo daigaku shuppan kai, 1981), 91–130. Having published *Nihon chūsei kaihatsu shi no kenkyū* (*A History of Medieval Japanese Land Development*) in 1984, Kuroda was at one time a strong advocate of the late Heian as a time of increased land clearance and improved farming. Since then he has given up the crusade to study pictorial sources such as scroll paintings and maps because, in the words of a younger colleague, "he sensed a limitation (dead end) in [his previous] research" (private conversation with Hongō Keiko, March 1999). When interviewed, Kuroda admits only that "the late Heian was a time when the *idea* of land clearance first became widespread" (interview with Kuroda Hideo, March 1999).

16. Kimura Shigemitsu, "Dai kaikon jidai no kaihatsu," in Miura Keiichi, ed., *Gijutsu no shakai shi 1 Kodai chūsei no gijutsu to shakai*, 150–204; also see his *Nihon kodai chūsei hatasaku shi no kenkyū* (Azekura shobo, 1992) and *Hatake to Nihonjin* (Chūkō shinsho, 1996).

17. One need merely peruse book reviews of Kimura's research to see the problems with applying this paradigm from Western Europe willy-nilly to twelfth-century Japan. Reviews of Kimura work were so critical that he was forced to write a not-too-convincing rebuttal. See Isogai Fujio, "Shohyō," *Rekishi hyōron* 524 (December 1993): 97–102; Kawane Yoshihira, "Shohyō to shōkai," *Nihon rekishi* 556 (September 1994): 113–15; Suzuki Tetsuo, "Shohyō," *Shikai* 36 (June 1993): 78–83; Takahashi Takashi, "Shohyō," *Rekishigaku kenkyū* 655 (February 1994): 43–45; Ihara Kesao, "Shohyō," *Shakai keizai shigaku* 60 (September 1994): 84–88; Kimura Shigemitsu, "Kenkyū nooto," *Jinmin no rekishigaku* 126 (January 1996): 30–36.

18. Umata Ayako, "Chūsei no hajimari," in *Aou shi shi* (Aou-shi kyōiku iinkai, 1984), 1:405–29, 710–18; for a recent critique of Umata's work, see Maeda Tetsushi, "Harima no kuni Akaho gun Hisatomi ho no kihon shiryō ni tsuite," *Matsukaneyama ronsō* 30 (1996): 31–54. Also note Kawane Yoshihira, "Izumi Kōnō ke monjo chū no Heian makki no monjo ni tsuite," *Ritsumeikan bungaku* 521 (June 1991): 120–25.

19. Isogai, "Shohyō," 97–98.

20. Kimura, "Chūsei zenki no nōgyō seisanryoku to hatasaku," 74–76; *Nihon kodai chūsei hatasaku shi no kenkyū*, 233–305; Nagasawa Hiroshi, "Chūseiteki jimoku toshite no hata no seiritsu," *Shigaku kenkyū* 152 (June 1981): 1–22.

21. Mizuno Shōji, *Nihon chūsei no sonraku to shōen sei* (Azekura shobō, 2000), 85–140, 216–25, 371–419.

22. Inagaki Yasuhiko, "Chūsei no nōgyō keiei to shūshu keitai," in *Iwanami kōza Nihon rekishi 6 Chūsei 2* (Iwanami shoten, 1975), 175–82. Also see Inagaki Yasuhiko, "Shoki myōden no kōzō," in Inagaki Yasuhiko and Nagahara Keiji, eds., *Chūsei no shakai to keizai* (Tokyo daigaku shuppan kai, 1962), 1–80.

23. Nagahara Keiji, *Nihon no chūsei shakai* (Iwanami shoten, 1968), 157–72; Yamamoto Takashi, *Shōen sei no tenkai to chiiki shakai* (Tosui shobō, 1995), 104–18.

24. Kuroda, *Chūsei kaihatsu shi*, 64–69, 97–142, 344–70.

25. Minegishi Sumio, *Onnabori: Chūsei shoki nōgyō yōsui shi hakkutsu chōsa;* "Onnabori," in *Tōsonshi* (Gendai shobō shinsha, 1979), 212–19. In his recent *Chūsei saigai senran no shakai shi* (Yoshikawa kōbunkan, 2001), Minegishi uses the phrase "age of widespread land clearance" and argues that the climate was favorable to that activity in the late eleventh and twelfth centuries, but then proceeds to describe an eruption of Mt. Asama during the same period and assert that the land clearance was merely the reopening of abandoned fields (pp. 25–63).

Also note Takahashi Manabu, "Kodai matsu ikō ni okeru chikei kankyō no henbō to tochi kaihatsu," *Nihon shi kenkyū* 380 (April 1994): 33–49, which points to archaeological evidence that many irrigation ditches deteriorated after 950.

26. Harada Nobuo, *Chūsei sonraku no keikan to seikatsu* (Kyoto: Shibunkaku, 1999), 22–23.

27. Nishiyachi and Iinuma, "Chūseiteki tochi shoyū," 82–83; Kitō Hiroshi, *Nihon nisen nen no jinkō shi* (PHP Paperbacks, 1983), 54–55.

28. For Nishiyachi and Iinuma, see Note 15; for Takahashi, see Note 25. Even Takahashi, it seems, envisions widespread land abandonment before the new round of field creation commenced after 1100.

29. Kinda Akihiro, *Kodai Nihon no keikan;* "Kokuzu no jōri puran to shōen no jōri puran," *Nihon shi kenkyū* 332 (April 1990): 1–35.

30. See, for instance, John Hall, *Government and Local Power in Japan, 500–1700* (Princeton: Princeton University Press, 1966), 86–87; 98, photograph 16; and Joan Piggott, "Sacral Kingship and Confederacy in Early Izumo," *Monumenta Nipponica* 44 (spring 1989): 63–66.

31. Uno, *Shōen no kōkogaku*, 63–68

32. Ishii Susumu, *Kamakura bushi no jitsuzō* (Heibon sha, 1987), 109.

33. Kuroda, *Chūsei kaihatsu shi*, 97–146; Kimura, "Chūsei zenki no nōgyō to hatasaku," 65–73; Nagasawa, "Chūseiteki jimoku toshite no hata no seiritsu," 1–22. Kuroda and Kimura note the conversion from unirrigated to irrigated cropping as well; see Kimura, *Hatake to Nihonjin*, 122–30.

34. Kuroda, *Chūsei kaihatsu shi*, 52–64.

35. Furushima, *Furushima Toshio chosaku shū*, 143–46; Morris, "Land and Society," 2:189–94. It should be noted that Kuroda assumes that the tools mentioned in his documents were made of iron (*Chūsei kaihatsu shi*, 41–52).

36. On rain-fed paddies, see Yagi Hironori, *Suiden nōgyō no hatten ronri* (Nihon hyōron keizai sha, 1983), 31–102; Kagose Yoshiaki, *Teishitchi* (Kokin shoin, 1972), 77–80; Saitō Osamu, "Inasaku to hatten no hikaku shi," in *Tōnan Ajia kara no chiteki bōken* (Libro, 1986), 200–25; Yamada Tatsuo, "Kinsei shōnōmin jiritsu no nōhōteki kiso," in *Nōhō tenkai no ronri* (Ochanomizu shobō, 1975), 3–24.

On the prevalence of dry fields, also see Amino Yoshihiko, *Nihon chūsei no minshū zō* (Iwanami shoten, 1980), 63–75; Kuroda, *Chūsei kaihatsu shi*, 97–146; Hatai Hiromu, "Nara Heian jidai no yakibata nōgyō," in *Chūsei shakai no seiritsu to tenkai* (Yoshikawa kōbunkan, 1976), 1–140; Itō Toshikazu, "Heian Kamakura jidai no yakibata ni kansuru rekishi chirigakuteki kenkyū," *Nihon joshi daigaku bungaku bu kiyō* 45 (1995): 79–96.

On other livelihoods, see Kagetsu Yoichiro, "Teijū," in *Nihon minzoku bunka taikei*

6 *Hyōhaku to teichaku* (Shōgakkan, 1984), 431–62.

37. Iyanaga Teizō, *Nara jidai no kizoku to nōmin* (Jibun dō, 1956), 169.

38. Kinda Akihiro, *Jōri to sonraku no rekishi chirigaku kenkyū* (Daimei dō, 1985), 339–487. For example, Shimo Uda, on the tip of western Honshu, was founded in the middle Heian as a tiny hamlet of only six small groups of dwellings. In the late Heian, it shrank to only four. Also note the case of Masukata in Dewa in Ono Masatoshi, *Zukai Nihon no chūsei iseki* (Tokyo daigaku shuppan kai, 2001), 44, 53.

39. Gina Barnes, *Protohistoric Yamato* (Ann Arbor: University of Michigan Press, 1988), 238–42; Kristina Troost, "Peasants, Elites, and Villages in the Fourteenth Century," in Jeffrey Mass, ed., *The Origins of Japan's Medieval World* (Stanford: Stanford University Press, 1997), 98–100; Morris, "Land and Society," 2:194–99.

40. Kinda Akihiro, *Bichikei to chūsei sonraku* (Yoshikawa kōbunkan, 1993).

41. The government's ban on moving was undoubtedly related to the scarcity of labor. See below. Also note Ishimoda Shō (*Nihon no kodai kokka* [Iwanami shoten, 1971], 343–48), who for this reason describes ancient Japanese society as a "generalized slave system" (*sōtaiteki dorei sei*).

42. Thomas Keirstead, *The Geography of Power in Medieval Japan* (Princeton: Princeton University Press, 1992), 34–38.

43. Hotate Michihisa, "Chūsei minshū keizai no tenkai," in *Kōza Nihon rekishi* 3 *Chūsei* 1 (Tokyo daigaku shuppan kai, 1984), 178; Suzuki Tetsuo, "Echigo no kuni Ishii no shō ni okeru 'kaihatsu' to rōnin," *Nihon shi kenkyū* 303 (November 1987): 30–47. Also see his *Chūsei Nihon no kaihatsu to hyakusei* (Iwata shoin, 2001), 43–96. For the record, Suzuki is also a critic of the "age of widespread land clearance"; see pp. 9–42.

44. An instructive parallel is Europe during the age of the plague, when the harshest legislation could not halt rural migration; see Harry Miskimin, *The Economy of Early Renaissance Europe, 1300–1460* (Cambridge: Cambridge University Press, 1975), 27, 30, 46. For a recent article on illegal migrants during the Nara period, see Ōmachi Ken, "Nihon kodai no furō seisaku ni okeru shozaichishugi to futatsu no honganchishugi," *Nihonshi kenkyū* 486 (February 2003): 1–26.

45. On these three levies, see the notes by Yoshida Takashi in *Ritsuryō* (Iwanami shoten, 1975), 3:249–61, 580–94. Commutation of these labor dues became common in the ninth century. For a brief discussion in English, see William Wayne Farris, *Sacred Texts and Buried Treasures: Issues in the Historical Archaeology of Ancient Japan* (Honolulu: University of Hawai'i Press, 1998), 191–94.

Also note that in March 2006, archaeologists excavating the Southern Gate (*rajō*) of Nara discovered that rather than a tamped-earth, tiled wall, the entrance was a simple fence, further supporting the argument made in *Sacred Texts and Buried Treasures* that construction at that capital suffered from constraints on time, materials, and labor; see "Heijō-kyō rajō kanryakuban ka," *Asahi shinbun*, March 15, 2006.

46. Yoshito Hakeda, *Kukai: Major Works* (New York: Columbia University Press, 1972), 54.

47. Ibid., 58.

48. Paul Groner, *Saichō: The Establishment of the Japanese Tendai School*, Buddhist Studies Series (Berkeley: Asian Humanities Press, 1985), 281.

49. Takinami Sadako, "Heian kyō no kōzō," in Sasayama Haruo, ed., *Kodai o kangaeru Heian no miyako* (Yoshikawa kōbunkan, 1991), 83–85; Katō Sadako, "Kyakusaku jiyaku no shiteki igi," *Kodai bunka* 27 (February 1975): 32–46.

50. Takinami, "Heian kyō no kōzō," 86–87; Aoki Kazuo, "Koeki sei no seiritsu," *Shigaku zasshi* 67 (April 1958): 52–53.

51. On this levy, see Kiley, "Provincial Administration and Land Tenure," 298–337; Ōtsu Tōru, *Ritsuryō kokka shihai kōzō no kenkyū* (Iwanami shoten, 1993), 284–348; Okuno Nakahiko, "Rinji zōyaku no seiritsu to tenkai," *Nihon rekishi* 255 (August 1969): 32–49; Sakamoto, *Ōchō kokka taisei*, 157–94, and *Sekkan jidai*, 126–61; and Kushiki Yoshinori, "Kokuga chōhatsu rikieki no kōzō to hensen," in *Nihon no zenkindai to Hokuriku shakai* (Kyoto: Shibunkaku, 1989), 101–32; "Heian jidai Kyoto ni okeru rikieki," *Hisutoria* 108 (September 1985): 1–16. It was not, as Dana Morris asserts in "Land and Society," 2:215, for example, "new" and additional.

52. Kiley, "Provincial Administration and Land Tenure," 320–21.

53. Ōtsu, *Ritsuryō kokka shihai kōzō*, 300–348; Matsubara Hironobu, "Shūrishiki ni tsuite no ichi kenkyū," *Hisutoria* 78 (March 1978): 1–22; Uejima Susumu, "Heian kōki kokka zaisei no kenkyū," *Nihon shi kenkyū* 360 (August 1992): 33–68.

54. Paul Groner, *Ryōgen and Mount Hiei* (Honolulu: University of Hawai'i Press, 2002), 167–72.

55. Mikael S. Adolphson, *The Gates of Power: Monks, Courtiers, and Warriors in Pre-Modern Japan* (Honolulu: University of Hawai'i Press, 2000), 47–48.

56. Sakamoto, *Sekkan jidai*, 253–62.

57. On finance and construction in this era, see Uejima Susumu, "Jōkō sei no tenkai," *Shirin* 75 (July 1992): 74–113; Kiley, "Provincial Administration and Land Tenure," 298–337; Ōtsu, *Ritsuryō kokka shihai kōzō*, 284–348; Sakamoto, *Ōchō kokka taisei*, 232–44, 326, and *Sekkan jidai*, 337–39; Uejima Susumu, "Heian kōki kokka zaisei no kenkyū," *Nihon shi kenkyū* 360 (August 1992): 33–68; Uejima Susumu, "Ikkoku heikin yaku no kakuritsu katei," *Shirin* 73 (January 1990): 41–72; Kushiki, "Kokuga chōhatsu rikieki," 120–25, and "Heian jidai Kyoto ni okeru rikieki," 1–16.

58. Uejima, "Heian kōki kokka zaisei," 36, 61.

59. Ōtsu, *Ritsuryō kokka shihai kōzō*, 316; *Honchō seiki*, Kōji 1/6/18, 373.

60. Sakamoto, *Sekkan jidai*, 360–65. Also note Maruyama Hitoshi, "Insei ki ni okeru goganji zōei jigyō," *Nenpō chūsei shi kenkyū* 26 (2001): 85–112, for more signs of a revival of construction in the late Heian epoch.

61. On iron metallurgy, I mainly relied upon *Nihon kodai no tetsu seisan* (Rokkō shuppan, 1991), 231–75; and Gotō Tadatoshi, "Ro no kōzō ni tsuite," in *Kodai Nihon no tetsu to shakai* (Heibon sha, 1982), 109–17. Ono, *Zukai Nihon no chūsei iseki*, 102–7; Isogawa Shin'ya, "Kodai chūsei no chūtetsu imono," *Kokuritsu rekishi minzoku hakubutsukan kenkyū kiyō* 46 (December 1992): 1–80; and Tosa Masahiko, "Nihon kodai seitetsu iseki ni kansuru kenkyū josetsu," *Tatara kenkyū* 24 (August 1981): 12–34; were also helpful. The best examples of furnaces come from the Kanto; see, for example, *Sōma kaihatsu kanren iseki chōsa hōkoku* 1: *Honbun* 1, 2 (Fukushima-shi: Fukushima-ken kyōiku iinkai, 1989 and 1991, respectively); and *Hara chō karyoku hatsuden sho kanren iseki chōsa hōkoku* 1, 3, 5, 7, 8 (Fukushima-shi: Fukushima-ken kyōiku iinkai, 1990, 1992, 1995, and 1998, respectively). It should be noted that most of these examples used airpipes, although a bellows has never been recovered.

62. *Nihon kodai no tetsu seisan*, 240. How this discussion fits with the development of iron metallurgy in China and Korea and the later evolution of the distinctive Japanese *tatara* awaits more systematic and intensive study.

63. On silk, I consulted *Meiji zen Nihon sangyō gijutsu shi* (Nihon gakujutsu shinkō kai, 1960), 3–7; and Itō Toshio, *Mono to ningen no bunka shi* 68–I *Kinu* (Hōsei daigaku

shuppan kyoku, 1992), 156–63.

64. For example, see selected laws listed in *Ruijū sandai kyaku* (Yoshikawa kōbunkan, 1936), 330–43, passim; Tsunoyama Yukihiro, "Kodai no senshoku," in *Kōza Nihon gijutsu no shakai shi 3 Bōseki* (Nihon hyōron sha, 1983), 21–35. Also note Carole Cavanaugh, "Text and Textile: Unweaving the Female Subject in Heian Writing," *Positions* 4 (winter 1996): 595–636, which maintains that women made most aristocratic silks.

65. Wakita Haruko, "Chūsei no kōtsū, un'yu," in *Kōza Nihon gijutsu no shakai shi 8 Kōtsū un'yu* (Nihon hyōron sha, 1985), 102.

66. Kanō Hisashi and Kinoshita Masashi, "Shio tetsu no seisan to kōnō," in Yagi Atsuru, ed., *Kodai no chihō shi 2 San'in nankai hen* (Asakura shoten, 1977), 172–92.

67. Ibid., 185–87.

68. Shiraishi Taichirō, "Chūsei yōgyō no rinmei," in *Kōza Nihon gijutsu no shakai shi 4 Yōgyō* (Nihon hyōron sha, 1984), 104–5, 112.

69. Ono, *Zukai Nihon no chūsei iseki*, 108–11.

70. On lacquer production as a labor-intensive activity, see Habu Junko, *Ancient Jomon of Japan* (Cambridge: Cambridge University Press, 2004), 220.

71. Kozo, "The Decline of the *Ritsuryō* System," 32–34; "The Growth of Commerce," in Kozo Yamamura, ed., *The Cambridge History of Japan* (Cambridge: Cambridge University Press, 1990), 3:351–56; "The Development of Za in Medieval Japan," *Business History Review* 47 (winter 1973): 438–65.

72. Yoshida Takashi, *Ritsuryō kokka to kodai no shakai* (Iwanami shoten, 1983), 289–348. Two more recent contributions by Kushiki Yoshinori are "Nagaya ōke no shōhi to ryūtsū keizai," *Kokuritsu rekishi minzoku hakubutsukan kenkyū hōkoku* 92 (February 2002): 7–34; and "Shōnin to shōgyō no hassei," in *Shin taikei Nihon shi 12 Ryūtsū keizai shi* (Yamakawa shuppan sha, 2002), 81–111.

73. *Nihon kiryaku* (Yoshikawa kōbunkan, 1929), Eikan 2/11/6, 152 (984); Eien 1/11/2, 163 (987). On this demonetization, a recent article is Inoue Masao, "Heian chūki no dōsen ryūtsū tozetsu to shichō kenryoku kakujū no mondai," *Shakai keizai shigaku* 66 (March 2000): 3–22.

74. Kamei Meitoku, "NisSō bōeki no tenkai," in *Iwanami kōza Nihon tsūshi 6 Kodai 5* (Iwanami shoten, 1993), 112–38. Also see the recent article by Watanabe Makoto, "Heian chūki bōeki kanri no kihon kōzō," *Nihonshi kenkyū* 489 (May 2003): 31–50.

75. For more details, see Ishii Kenji, *Nihon no fune* (Sōgen sha, 1957), 76–118.

76. The quotation comes from Yamamura, "The Growth of Commerce," 347. From 1050, stories describing the wealth of merchants in Kyoto and other places appear with more frequency; see Karl Friday, *Samurai, Warfare, and the State in Early Medieval Japan* (New York and London: Routledge Press, 2004), 67 and 181, notes 21, 22.

77. Yamamura, "The Growth of Commerce," 344–60; Sasaki Gin'ya, "Sangyō no bunka to chūsei shōgyō," in Nagahara Keiji, ed., *Nihon keizai shi taikei 2 Chūsei* (Tokyo daigaku shuppan kai, 1965), 143–88. At the same time, it is interesting to note the great variety of dues from estates in the middle and late Heian periods, a fact perhaps compensating for the modest degree of commercial and monetary development; see Thomas Mesner, "Lamp Oil, Miso, and Moss: The Variety of Estate Revenues in the Heian Period," *Journal of Intercultural Studies* 20 (1993): 14–24.

78. Kishi Toshio, *Kodai kyūto no tankyū* (Hanawa shobō, 1984), 152–69, for the population of Nara. Provincial capitals are estimated to have had about 600 officials; therefore a population of 1,000 seems conservative but acceptable; see Ha-

yakawa Shōhachi, *Nihon no rekishi 3 Ritsuryō kokka* (Shōgakkan, 1974), 195–96. There was clearly a grid layout for Naniwa, and it was an important port; a population of 35,000, or about one-half of Nara, seems reasonable; see Nakao Yoshiharu, *Kōkogaku no raiburari-*, 46 *Naniwa no miyako* (Nyū saiensu sha, 1986). The remaining 15,000 are the residents of Dazaifu, a major transoceanic port.

79. William McCullough, "The Capital and Its Society," in Shively and McCullough, eds., *The Cambridge History of Japan*, 2:119–23. For an article examining the early layout of Heian using archaeological evidence, see Yamada Kunikazu, "'Zenki Heian-kyō' no fukugen," in Niki Hiroshi, ed., *Toshi: zenkindai toshi ron no shatei* (Aoki shoten, 2002), 107–38.

80. On the burning of Dazaifu, see Takeuchi Rizō, "Kodai no shūen," in Kagamiyama Takeshi and Tamura Enchō, eds., *Kodai no Nihon 3 Kyushu* (Kadokawa shoten, 1970), 353–56; on the end of Naniwa, see Nakao, *Kōkogaku no raiburari-*, 16–17.

81. On the *kokufu*, see "Kokufu kenkyū no genjō—sono ni," *Kokuritsu rekishi minzoku hakubutsukan kenkyū hōkoku* 20 (March 1989): 278–384; Takahashi Yasuo et al., eds., *Zushū Nihon toshi shi* (Tokyo daigaku shuppan kai, 1993), 76–77; Yoshie Akira, "Kokufu kara yadomachi e," *Rekishi to bunka* 16 (1988): 118–68; Yoshie Akira, "Chūsei zenki no kokufu," *Kokuritsu rekishi minzoku hakubutsukan kenkyū hōkoku*, 8 (December 1985): 23–101; Ogawa Makoto, *Chūsei toshi 'fuchū' no tenkai* (Shibunkaku, 2001).

82. Kamei, "NisSō bōeki no tenkai," 119–40; Yamamura Shin'ei, "Chūsei Dazaifu no tenkai," in *Chūsei toshi kenkyū 4 Toshi to shūkyō* (Shin jinbutsu ōrai sha, 1997), 65–86.

83. Yamamura, "The Growth of Commerce," 356–60; on Hiraizumi, see Mimi H. Yiengpruksawan, *Hiraizumi* (Council on East Asian Studies, Harvard University, 1998); and Irumada Nobuo and Tomiyama Kazuyuki, *Kita no Hiraizumi, minami no Ryukyu* (Chūō kōron sha, 2002), 15–164. On overall urban population, see Kitō Hiroshi, *Edo jidai no jinkō to shakai* (Jōchi daigaku, 1990), 77–78, where Kitō estimates that in 1590 only about 5 percent of Japan's population dwelt in towns of 5,000 residents or more. While city-dwellers in 1150 may have numbered more than 200,000, it seems unlikely that it would have been much greater, given Japan's pattern of pre-1600 urban development.

84. Morris, "Land and Society," 2:197, gives an average for the *bōko* (about 8–10); William Wayne Farris, *Population, Disease, and Land in Early Japan, 645–900* (Council on East Asian Studies, Harvard University, 1985), 26–34, uses data divided into *gōko* (25–30). The larger *gōko* was the only unit until 715, when the court initiated a reform of the village that entailed creating more households, known as *bōko*, within the old households *(gōko)*. To make the situation even more confusing, after 715 registers record both types of households. Archaeological remains of pit dwellings could house 2–8 members, but scholars have no way of knowing how many pit dwellings a family lived in. Yoshida Takashi (*Taikei Nihon no rekishi 3 Kodai kokka no ayumi* [Shōgakkan, 1988], 248) opts for an average household of 5 members, but he assumes that each family was restricted to a single pit dwelling. This issue requires further research; also see Introduction, notes 19 and 20.

85. Farris, *Population, Disease, and Land*, 44–47.

86. Yoshida, *Kodai kokka no ayumi*, 245–53. Yoshida bases his reasoning at least in part on *Sosō-ryō no shūge, Fukki no jō*, 971–73. For more examples, note Yoshida, "Ritsuryō sei to sonraku," 160. Also see Yoshie Akiko, *Nihon kodai no uji no kōzō* (Yoshikawa kōbunkan, 1986); and Sumi Tōyō, *Zenkindai Nihon kazoku no kōzō* (Kōbun

dō, 1983). Yoshie has recently expressed her views in English; see "Gender in Early Classical Japan," *Monumenta Nipponica* 60 (winter 2005): 438–79.

One major exception to this rule is Tsude, *Nihon nōkō shakai no seiritsu katei*, 442–65, which advocates patrilineal kinship. A more recent study interpreting the household registers as supporting patrilineal kinship is Imazu Katsunori, "Nihon kodai no sonraku to chiiki shakai," *Kōkogaku kenkyū* 50 (December 2003): 57–74. It may be criticized, however, for taking the households listed in the registers as real family units *(jittai setsu)*. Also see Emori Itsuo, "Kon'in keitai to shūzoku," in Ōbayashi Taryō, ed., *Nihon no kodai* 11 *Uji to ie* (Chūō kōron sha, 1987), 111–58, which proposes that both bilateral and patrilineal customs were observed in different parts of the islands.

87. See Kōmoto Masayuki, "Yayoi jidai no shakai," in Sahara Makoto and Kanaseki Hiroshi, eds., *Kodai shi hakkutsu 4 Inasaku no hajimari* (Kōdan sha, 1975), 87–98. For a short English-language treatment, see Farris, *Sacred Texts and Buried Treasures*, 26–28.

88. Robin Fox, *Kinship and Marriage,* (Harmondsworth: Penguin Books, 1967), 83.

89. *Ko-ryō no shūge, ōbun no jō, koki*, 293. There is much Japanese research on this article and the ancient system of inheritance. See, for example, Nakata Kaoru, "Yōrō ko-ryō ōbun jō no kenkyū," *Hōsei shi ronshū* (Iwanami shoten, 1926), 1:43–83; Inoue Tatsuo, "Ko-ryō ōbun jō no seiritsu," in *Nihon kodai shi ronshū* (Yoshikawa kōbunkan, 1962), 2:129–76; and Miyamoto Tasuku, "Nihon kodai kazoku hō no shiteki ichikōsatsu," *Kodai gaku* 3 (December 1954): 366–84.

90. It should be noted that while *kubunden* was not heritable, household lots and newly reclaimed land were usually personal possessions and subject to inheritance.

91. In the following discussion, "duolocal" is used when husband and wife maintain separate residences; "uxorilocal" means that the husband lived with the wife's family, and "neolocal" indicates that the married couple found a new residence away from either set of parents. In English, the classic study is William McCullough, "Japanese Marital Institutions in the Heian Period," *Harvard Journal of Asiatic Studies* 27 (1967): 103–67.

According to Sekiguchi Hiroko, spouses were not even buried together; see her "Nihon kodai ni okeru fūfu gōsō no ippanteki fuzai," *Seisen joshi daigaku jinbun kagaku kenkyū kiyō* 22 (2001): 147–90.

92. For *The Chronicles of Japan*, see *Nihongi: Chronicles of Japan from the Earliest Times to A.D. 697*, translated by William Aston (London: Kegan, Trench, and Trubner, 1896), 2:220 (Taika 2/3/22). For the original, see *Nihon shoki*, edited by Sakamoto Tarō et al. (Iwanami shoten, 1965), Taika 2/3/22, 294–95. Scholars differ on whether the gifts were indeed what anthropologists mean by "bridewealth." Yoshida, *Kodai kokka no ayumi*, 238–40, adheres to the negative position, while Emori Itsuo, "Kon'in keitai to shūzoku," in Ōbayashi, ed., *Nihon no kodai* 11 *Uji to ie* (Chūō kōron sha, 1987), 138–40, supports the positive.

93. Takamure Itsue, *Nihon kon'in shi* (Jibun dō, 1963), 105–10. Referring to a collection of late eleventh-century stories known as *Tales of Times Now Past (Konjaku monogatari shū)*, Takamure counted 287 instances of marriage, and of those 61 showed clearly where the "marriage" started: 30 took place in the wife's parents' home, and 31 involved a neolocal residence. Never did the wife go to her husband's parents' living quarters to reside, which was common later in the more patriarchal Edo period. Takamure also divided the families into three types: complex, simple, and broken. Thirty-four of 41 complex families resided in the woman's parents' house, about half

the nuclear families lived with the wife's relatives, and almost all broken families dwelled with the mother. Complex families included not just parents and children but also other relatives of the husband or wife; simple families refer to nuclear arrangements; broken families were headed by a single parent with offspring.

To be sure, Takamure's work has come under increasing criticism in recent decades. For example, one scholar reexamined the stories in *Tales of Times Now Past* and concluded that the wife's parents were not nearly so powerful as Takamure had believed; this younger female researcher suggested that among peasants marriage usually involved only the young man and woman, who then relocated to a new house. The style of marriage Takamure had termed "take-in-the-husband" existed but was not nearly as widespread as previously posited. When the newlyweds relocated, in most cases the woman followed the man; see Nishimura Hiroko, *"Konjaku monogatari ni okeru kon'in keitai to kon'in kankei," Rekishi hyōron* 335 (March 1978): 39–53, or her *Kodai chūsei kazoku to josei* (Yoshikawa kōbunkan, 2002), 228–52. Sekiguchi Hiroko (*Nihon kodai kon'in shi no kenkyū* [Hanawa shobō, 1993], 2:3–200) seems to agree with Nishimura on the importance of neolocal marriage. Hitomi Tonomura ("Black Hair and Red Trousers: Gendering the Flesh in Medieval Japan," *The American Historical Review* 99 [February 1994]: 129–54; and "Re-envisioning Women in the Post-Kamakura Age," in Jeffrey Mass, ed., *The Origins of Japan's Medieval World* [Stanford: Stanford University Press, 1997], 138–69) appear to be revising Takamure's views.

94. Yoshida, *Kodai kokka no ayumi*, 240–42.

95. Ibid., 236–45.

96. Emori, "Kon'in keitai to shūzoku," 140–43.

97. Takamure, *Kon'in shi,* 98–105; Morris, "Land and Society," 2:194–99. In Morris' view, Heian peasant families comprised 8–10 members. It should be noted that he made this assertion for duolocal marriage. On the variety and importance of women's labor in ancient Japan, see Yoshie, "Gender in Early Classical Japan," 446–65.

98. See Kenneth Hall, "Economic History of Early Southeast Asia," in Nicholas Tarling, ed., *The Cambridge History of Southeast Asia* (Cambridge: Cambridge University Press, 1992), 1:190–91.

99. Kōchi Shōsuke, "Taihō-ryō handen shūju seido kō," *Shigaku zasshi* 86 (March 1977): 1–39. Also asserting the dangers of birth and high infant mortality rates is Moriyama Shigeki and Nakae Kazue, *Nihon kodomo shi* (Heibon sha, 2002), 63–71, 80–88.

100. See Sawada Goichi, *Nara chō jidai minsei keizai no sūteki kenkyū* (Kashiwa shobō, 1972), 295. Also note Yamamura, "The Decline of the *Ritsuryō* System," 30–32, for an interpretation that argues for a scarcity of labor as the major factor in the rise and collapse of slavery. It is true, as Yamamura states, that slaves tended to disappear by the tenth century, but it is difficult to tell much about social structure of middle and late Heian Japan because of the aforementioned dearth of sources.

101. Hirai Kiyoshi, *Zusetsu Nihon jūtaku no rekishi* (Gakugei shuppan sha, 1980), 5–22; *Nihon jūtaku no rekishi* (NHK bukkusu, 1974), 8–36, 208–19.

102. Nishitani Tadashi, "Kara chiiki to hokubu Kyushu," in *Dazaifu ko bunka ronsō* (Yoshikawa kōbunkan, 1983), 1:36–46; Hayashi Hiromichi, "Kamado shutsugen ni kansuru ni san mondai," in *Mizu to tsuchi no kōkogaku* (Jōyō-shi: Kōyū kai, 1973), 95–110.

103. Hirai, *Zusetsu,* 5–22. Yoshida, "Ritsuryō sei to sonraku," 145–47, mentions

the more advanced housing in the Kinai. Note that many scholars believe that these large "posthole" *(hottate bashira)* structures belonged to local magnates such as the district magistrates; see *Takatsuki shi shi: Kōko hen* (Takatsuki-shi: Takatsuki-shi, 1973), 6:104–13, for the first of these sites, called *Gūke Kawanishi iseki.*

104. Hirai, *Zusetsu,* 5–22.

105. Yoshida, "Ritsuryō sei to sonraku," 147.

106. Nagahara Keiji, "Chūsei kinsei ikōki no gijutsu seisanryoku no hatten," *Kokushigaku ronshū* (Imai Rintarō sensei kijū kinen ronbun shū kankō kai, 1988), 235.

107. Sekine Masataka, *Nara chō shoku seikatsu no kenkyū* (Yoshikawa kōbunkan, 1969), 429–35.

108. Ibid., 443–48. Also see Maruyama Yumiko, *Tenpyō no hikari to kage* (Nihon hōsō shuppan kyokai, 1999), 156–64.

109. Susan Hanley, *Everyday Things in Premodern Japan* (Berkeley: University of California Press, 1997), 104–28. In most cases, toilets were either wooden buckets or simple latrines complete with two parallel boards upon which the person squatted; see *Toire no kōkogaku* (Tokyo bijutsu, 1997), 21–40. Cleaning toilets was the job of the lowly and may not have been done thoroughly or frequently. Moreover, the earliest toilets indicate the existence of parasite eggs in the intestines of the users; see Gina Barnes and Masaaki Okita, "Japanese Archaeology in the 1990s," *Journal of Archaeological Research* 7: (1999) 354–55.

110. Takahashi Masaaki, "Yogore no Kyoto, goryō e, bushi," *Atarashii rekishigaku no tame ni* 199 (July 1990): 3; Yasuda Masahiko, "Heian-kyō no nioi," in Hashimoto Yoshimasa, ed., *Kankyō rekishi no shiza* (Iwata shoin, 2002), 135–60.

111. Takahashi, "Yogore no Kyoto," 6.

112. McCullough, "The Capital and Its Society," 152.

CONCLUSION

This book has examined the population of ancient Japan from many angles. Its chief goals were to present an overview of the historiography of the topic; derive justifiable estimates for three eras (the second quarter of the eighth, the mid-tenth, and the mid-twelfth centuries); and fit the trend so inferred with numerous variables, including ones directly affecting the population such as pestilence and famine and background factors such as agrarian technology, the labor market, and material culture. Even though I have considered many components of population change, I hope that readers will view this work not as the last word on the subject, but rather as a hypothesis to be tested and discussed as more evidence becomes available. It is hard to believe that other major sources or new ways around the assumptions of the various methods employed here are readily available; certainly in the future scholars should conduct research on migration, the labor market, various industries, urbanization, the family and marriage, and the physical well-being of the populace in more detail and their data may well result in more authoritative results.

Concerning the historiographical review, I showed that while scholars evinced an early interest in Japan's early population, few estimates made prior to 1945 are reliable. Yokoyama Yoshikiyo made three calculations for the ninth and tenth centuries in 1879, but except for the mid-tenth century, serious flaws beset them all. The same may also be said of Kimura Masakoto's tally for the tenth century. Only Sawada Goichi, who estimated mid-eighth century population at 6–7 million, made a long-lasting contribution to this field before 1945.

After World War II, the newfound freedom to examine Japan's ancient history critically benefited those who wanted to know more about demography. Urata Akiko determined that the "household" of the census records was an administrative fiction devised to raise more conscripts. The archeological boom aided, too, first of all by allowing Koyama Shūzō to infer his demographic cycle for the Jōmon and then by providing the skeletal evidence for Kobayashi Kazumasa to derive life expectancies for the same period.

To Kitō Hiroshi fell the job of synthesizing most prior research and calculating new estimates for the Yayoi era, as well as the eighth, ninth, tenth, and twelfth centuries. His figures, computed in 1983, showed dramatic growth from the inception of the Yayoi until about 700, with a gradual leveling off thereafter. More significantly, his work seemed to contradict the conventional wisdom that population expanded greatly during the 700s, as purportedly implied by vigorous activity in land clearance at that time.

In addition to Kitō in the 1980s, Dana Morris studied the Heian household and argued that its large size arose from the need for more field hands. I inferred vital statistics for four sets of early eighth-century population data, suggesting that birth and death rates were high; infant mortality was at least 50 percent to age five, leading to an average life expectancy at birth of around twenty-five. Moreover, based on a finding by William McNeill, I endorsed the view that foreign-borne epidemics cut repeatedly and heavily into Japan's population after 700, reducing or perhaps even reversing growth. Ann Jannetta refined this thesis by suggesting that smallpox had become endemic in the archipelago earlier than McNeill or I had envisioned.

Later in the decade, Hanihara Kazurō quantified the expansion of the Yayoi and Tomb periods and indicated that in-migration from the Asian mainland greatly assisted the trend. The chance discovery of a lacquer-covered census record in Ibaraki bolstered the case for Sawada's 6–7 million figure for late eighth-century Japan. Kitō nicely brought this line of research to a climax by revising his findings in 2000, integrating more material and recalculating as he wrote.

Referring to these previous attempts, this essay has aimed at deriving a new set of estimates for early eighth, mid-tenth, and mid-twelfth century Japan. For the eighth century, I rejected Kamata's ingenious but flawed effort and instead followed what I believe was Sawada's original intent—that his estimate apply to Shōmu's reign (724–49). Utilizing data for the period 715–39, as well as computations taking into consideration Kamata's, Kitō's, and Sawada's contributions, I estimated Japan's population at 5.8–6.4 million around 730.

Sawada also made calculations for the early ninth and tenth centuries: 5.0–5.6 million in each case. Although there is, of course, the possibility that these figures significantly understate the real population, higher ones would present numerous difficulties, among which are the lack of a firm documentary basis and less room for growth during the late Heian or medieval eras. I decided on a range of 4.4–5.6 million for the mid-tenth century. The lower figure is Yokoyama's, while to obtain the higher number I modified Kitō's method derived from the paddy totals in *Wamyō shō*. I made two calculations, using in each a higher and more realistic figure for the rice acreage needed to sustain an individual: 2.17 *tan*. In the first computation, I assumed that the rice field totals represented all economic activity in the countryside, while in the second, I considered *Wamyō shō*'s numbers to cover only real rice production and integrated considerations such as the area of abandoned land included in the official numbers and a procedure for deriving the population not engaged in paddy farming. The tally for urban residents, the unregistered, and slaves was added to both computations.

Finally, I estimated a population of 5.5–6.3 million for 1150 based on the land figures found in *Shūgai shō*, once again utilizing the two methods described for inferring the population in 950. While doubts—such as the rice acreage necessary to support an individual or the diversity of occupations—may be entertained about these methods, they are the most reliable and accurate available, given the dearth of data for the late Heian epoch. This estimate is slightly less than or about the same as a similar figure for the early eighth century, implying that the late Heian period was still part of the declining or static phase of Japan's second major demographic cycle. At the same time, it is higher than the one I derived for the mid-tenth century, suggesting a modest improvement in living conditions between 950 and 1150.

Calculations done in this manner therefore show a stable or even slightly declining population from 700 to 1150. The final task was to determine what could have accounted for such an outcome. Among mortality factors, which directly affect growth, I added considerable new evidence to bolster the McNeill thesis, namely that repeated outbreaks of lethal epidemics had cut deeply into the population. These included deriving three more estimates for mortality from pestilence during the early eighth, late ninth, and late tenth centuries, respectively; presenting several examples of the effects of disease in estates in the eleventh; describing epidemics in the twelfth; discussing the quantities of archaeological evidence suggesting the effects of epidemics on the ritual life of the populace; and inferring the continuation of those effects until at least 1100 in the "departed spirit" rite *(goryō-e)*. The effect of these infectious outbreaks was also visible in elite artistic output. As Kitō also eventually admitted, a major reason for the static or diminishing population computed above was the impact of infectious disease in what McNeill has aptly called Japan's "age of microparasitism."

Important as pestilence was, a single factor is inadequate to explain or reinforce the curve adumbrated above. Famine was another frequent problem over this period, although the sources are much more telling for the eighth and ninth centuries. In those two centuries, crops in one or another area of Japan failed once every three years on average, induced by a combination of factors: drought, soil exhaustion, the near-absence of adequate irrigation facilities, and the lack of water-retaining woodland. Food shortages led to chronic or recurrent malnutrition for large segments of the population and famine produced its "season of death" in the early spring and summer, when stored food supplies gave out. Crop failure was also common in the early to mid-twelfth century, but the cause was most likely cold, damp summers. War and political instability were minor factors in mortality in general, although the Kanto peasants chased from their lands by Taira no Masakado or Tadatsune would not have so attested. The modest scale of violence notwithstanding, the tax base contracted noticeably in the ninth and tenth centuries, lending credence to the view that the number of taxpayers and probably the total population was declining.

Turning to farming practices and settlement patterns, factors that indirectly affect fertility and longevity or otherwise define demographic trends, we noted the high percentages of land out of cultivation from the mid-eighth century on. By the tenth and eleventh centuries, governors regularly assumed that at least 10 percent of rice paddies had gone to waste. Wealthier farmers adapted a new harness and plow system of tillage to substitute for the dearth of manual laborers and take advantage of more land for grazing. All in all, rural Japan between 900 and 1100 appears to have been a landscape with distinctly fewer signs of human occupancy than a century or so earlier.

While there may have been a modest increase in arable as a result of the "age of widespread land clearance" in the late eleventh and twelfth centuries, peasants redeveloped most fields from earlier ages. The area of dry fields may have grown, but their per unit yield was still low and they tended to go in and out of cultivation just like wet-rice paddies. The few figures available suggest that per unit harvests of rice barely increased over the eighth-century level. Greater utilization of the ox-drawn plow as well as more general dispersion of iron tools were minor improvements in the agrarian regime. Settlement and migration patterns fed into population trends in complex ways, but it is worth noting that scattered villages probably increased the time necessary for diseases to become endemic and internal migration may well have risen to a flood tide.

The labor market and industry also described and influenced demographic trends in many ways. In general, these sectors evinced a pattern of population decline because (1) insofar as we can tell, wages rose; and (2) several major ceremonial and religious projects remained unfinished or were undertaken only at infrequent intervals. Finally, six industries showed marked tendencies toward labor-saving conveniences and methods or outright retrogression. Both trade and urbanization reveal similar signs over the era 800–950, with commerce becoming demonetized and several towns shrinking. By the twelfth century, a modest rebound had occurred in both commerce and urbanization. The dynamism of the Sung dynasty played a critical role in remonetizing and aiding in the creation of port cities such as Hakata and Hyōgo.

Kinship, marriage, and the family can tell demographers about fertility and infant mortality, but unfortunately the only quantitative figures are those from the early 700s, and these are very high: about 45–50 births per 1,000 with about half the infants surviving beyond age five. To the extent that we know about these factors, descriptive sources must suffice. They reveal that kinship was bilateral, a practice that may have encouraged a high birth rate by spreading the population more evenly over the land. Partible inheritance was the prevailing custom, which probably meant that there was little pressure on land resources. Marriage among commoners was not marked by any distinctive ceremony, and liaisons were loose and free, perhaps resulting in frequent pregnancies. Spouses either lived separately or the male went to reside with his in-laws. Some see a shortage of labor as one reason for the latter living arrangement. Given these facts, fertility may well have been as high as noted above, but the numerous epidemics and famines undoubtedly served to lower the birth rate and raise infant mortality over long periods.

Finally, this monograph examined material well-being for the commoner class. In general, housing was the dank, cold, fire-prone pit dwelling; clothing was made of hemp or ramie and provided little warmth and comfort. Diet is a point about which controversy swirls, but it seems likely that it was merely adequate in the best of times. Cities like Kyoto or Nara were highly unsanitary, making them breeding grounds for the microbes that killed so many people.

In sum, although scholars may differ with the specific statistics presented here, it seems that a static or somewhat declining population between 700 and 1150 best fits the myriad factors we have considered above. Whether we look at the development of various labor-saving devices, the high incidence of wasted fields, the terrible mortality from epidemics as supplemented by famine, dwindling tax receipts, rising wages, and various other measures, all seem to confirm the demographic trend evinced above. We should recall Miyoshi Kiyoyuki's statement in 914: One can "understand the emptiness of the realm like the palm of one's hand."

These scraps of evidence and general trends all act to reinforce the conclusion reached by Kitō almost twenty years ago: that the era 700–1150 was a time of population stasis or even decline, the downside of his second cycle. The reader may, if he or she so chooses, bemoan this fact, but actually even decline has its uses. After all, if the population of the Japanese archipelago had not undergone the horrors and suffering inherent in the repeated outbreaks of pestilence, it would have built up no immunities. Japan would then have been left to the same fate as Native Americans or Hawaiian islanders some five hundred years later when the Iberians appeared. Put in economic terms, the formation of antigens in Japanese bodies was an investment in human capital, which once made, would pay dividends later on.[1] We may also view developments in agriculture, industry, and commerce as paving the way for growth in later epochs.

To return to the 1134–35 influenza bout, it has been described as the quintessential epidemic of the ancient period. But in some respects—the unusually cold weather, the widespread famine, the social upheaval, the suffering in Kyoto—it was also a harbinger of things to come. In this sense, the mid-twelfth century was a transitional time in Japanese history. These distinctive aspects combined with the old and the familiar to make the next era both the end of something old and the beginning of something new.

NOTE

1. James Nakamura, "Human Capital Accumulation in Premodern Rural Japan," *The Journal of Economic History* 41 (June 1981): 263–81.

A Brief Discussion of the Sources
Wamyō shō and *Shūgai shō*

According to the preface of *Wamyō ruijū shō*, Minamoto Shitagō compiled the dictionary during the 930s at the direction of Princess Kinshi, consort of Emperor Daigo. It contains more than 6,000 entries in Chinese and mixed Chinese-Japanese style. Originally there were 40 volumes *(maki)*, but today only two versions have come down to posterity, one of 10 and another of 20 volumes. *Wamyō shō* begins with a section about the heavens and sky, moves to the earth, then plants and trees, and so forth. It refers to more than 290 other sources and covers topics as diverse as courtly rituals, offices, and the names of provinces, districts, and administrative villages. Linguists suggest that the readings and terminology are close to those in use during the mid-tenth century.

Scholars have expressed doubts about Shitagō's authorship, however, since the Tokugawa period. In particular, the names of the districts and administrative villages listed in the twentieth volume often refer to appellations common during the eighth century, and some argue that they were written down as early as 925. As Iyanaga Teizō has pointed out in an interpretation that has now become widely accepted, the figures for arable land probably date from a somewhat later era, especially as the text betrays evidence of some emendations. In any case, I follow Iyanaga and most Japanese scholarly opinion that the arable data contained in *Wamyō shō* is a fairly accurate reflection of cultivation conditions as they existed around 950.[1]

Tradition also has it that Tōin Kinkata (1291–1360) drew up *Shūgai shō* in 1341. More recent scholarship, however, has concluded that the encyclopedia and guidebook for civil aristocrats probably took something near its present form around 1294 and then Tōin Sanehiro (1409–57?) revised and supplemented the manuscript. Yet the text also refers to the reign of Emperor Go-Horikawa in the early thirteenth century. Altogether, *Shūgai shō* is composed of three volumes and covers ninety-five topics, including daily rituals, musical instruments, court offices, Shinto shrines, and numerous maps of the palace and capital. In its day, *Shūgai shō* was a considered a basic handbook for the education and training of civil aristocrats.

According to Iyanaga, however, Kinkata clearly utilized much earlier dictionaries and encyclopedias from the late Heian period in listing provincial totals for arable. Like *Wamyō shō*, Tōin's work contains place names for districts and provinces, and it is likely that the author compiled the place names and data on arable separately from the body of the work. *Shūgai shō's* data on arable land are strikingly close to another encyclopedia, *Iroha jirui shō*, and it is thought they may have both been copied from the same older source, but because *Shūgai shō* lists total arable for all Japan while the other does not, it is presumed to be older and more authentic.[2]

Finally, when Iyanaga compared the arable numbers for *Wamyō shō* and *Shūgai shō*, he concluded that they are based on completely different sources. The former seems to be a fairly authentic representation of arable during the mid-tenth century; the latter seems to reflect conditions in the mid-twelfth century. The value of this information for determining all sorts of quantitative questions, such as progress in land clearance or population change, is high indeed.

NOTES

1. Iyanaga Teizō, *Kodai shakai keizai shi* (Iwanami shoten, 1980), 353–55.
2. Ibid., 363–67.

Appendix Table. Arable Totals for Japan's Provinces

Province	Wamyō shō	Shūgai shō
Kinai		
1.Yamashiro	8,961.7.290	8,961
2.Yamato	17,905.9.180	17,005.70
3.Kawachi	11,338.4.160	10,977
4.Izumi	4,569.6.357	4,126
5.Settsu	12,525.0.178	11,314
Tōkaidō		
6.Iga	4,051.1.041	4,055
7.Ise	18,130.6.245	19,024
8.Shima	124.0.094	4,917
9.Owari	6,820.7.310	11,930
10.Mikawa	6,820.7.310	7,054
11.Tōtōmi	13,611.3.035	12,967
12.Suruga	9,063.2.165	9,797
13.Izu	2,110.4.112	2,814
14.Kai	12,249.9.258	10,043
15.Sagami	11,236.1.091	11,486
16.Musashi	35,574.7.096	51,540
17.Awa	4,335.8.059	4,362
18.Kazusa	22,846.9.235	22,666
19.Shimōsa	26,432.6.234	33,000
20.Hitachi	40,092.6.112	42,038
Tōsandō		
21.Ōmi	33,402.5.184	33,450
22.Mino	14, 823.1.065	45,304
23.Hida	6,615.7.004	4,356
24.Shinano	30,908.8.140	30,520
25.Kōzuke	30,937.0.144	28,453
26.Shimotsuke	30,155.8.004	27,460

Province	Wamyō shō	Shūgai shō
27.Mutsu	51,440. 3.099	45,077
28.Dewa	26,109.2.051	38,628.5
Hokurikudō		
29.Wakasa	3,077.4.048	3,139
30.Echizen	12,066	23,576
31.Kaga	13,766.7.334	12,536
32.Noto	8,205.8.236	8,479
33.Etchū	17,909.5.030	21,399
34.Echigo	14,997.5.207	23,738
35.Sado	3,960.4	4,870
San'indō		
36.Tanba	10,666.0.262	10,855
37.Tango	4,756.0.155	5,537
38.Tajima	7,555.8.005	7,743
39.Inaba	7,914.8.208	8,016
40.Hōki	8,161.6.088	8,842
41.Izumo	9,435.8.285	9,968
42.Iwami	4,884.9.042	4,872
43.Oki	585.2.342	624
Sanyōdō		
44.Harima	21,414.3.036	21,236
45.Mimasaka	11,021.3.256	11,616
46.Bizen	13,185.7.032	13,206
47. Bitchū	10,227.8.252	10,883
48. Bingo	9,301.2.046	9,298
49.Aki	7,357.8.047	7,484
50.Suō	7,834.3.269	7,657
51.Nagato	4,603.4.231	4,769

Province	Wamyō shō	Shūgai shō
Nankaidō		
52.Kii	7,198.5.100	7,119
53.Awaji	2,650.9.160	2,870
54.Awa	3,414.5.055	5,245
55.Sanuki	18,647.5.266	17,943
56.Iyo	13,501.4.006	14,825
57. Tosa	6,451.0.008	6,173
Saikaidō		
58.Chikuzen	18,500+	19,765
59.Chikugo	12,800+	11,377
60.Hizen	13,900+	13,462
61.Higo	13,900+	23,462
62.Buzen	13,200+	13,221
63.Bungo	7,500+	7,570
64.Hyūga	4,800+	8,298
65.Ōsumi	4,800+	4,707
66.Satsuma	4,800+	5,521
67.Iki	620	620
68.Tsushima	428	620

Source: For *Wamyō shō*, I followed *Shohon shūsei Wamyō shō: honbun hen*, 602–11; for *Shūgai shō*, I used the figures found in Iyanaga Teizō, *Nihon kodai shakai keizai shi kenkyū*, 380–83. Note that population estimates using these arable figures and the second demographic method described in Chapter 1 may be found in Table 5. For convenience sake, in estimating the populations, I rounded all areas to the nearest *chō*.

CHARACTER LIST

akusō 悪僧

banjin 万人
bōko 房戸

chō 町
Chūyūki 中右記

daieki 大疫
dai kaikon jidai 大開墾時代
dairi 内裏
denso 田租
doba 土馬

eki 駅
ekishin 疫神
Engi shiki 延喜式

fukanden den 不堪佃田
fuko 封戸
furōnin 浮浪人

gisei setsu 擬制説
gō 郷
gōko 郷戸
gōri 郷里
goryō-e 御霊会
Gozu tennō 牛頭天王
gun 郡

haguchi 羽口
hakogata 箱型
handen sei 班田制
han chika shiki tategata ro
　半地下式竪型炉
Heian ibun 平安遺文

hitogata 人形
hottate bashira 掘立柱
Hyakuren shō 百練抄

ie 家
Iken jūnikajō 意見十二箇条
ikkoku heikin yaku 一国平均役
ishika no tateba 猪鹿の立庭

ji'nin 神人
jinmen bokusho doki 人面墨書土器
jittai setsu 実態説
jōden 上田
jōkō sei 成功制
jōri sei 条里制

kaito 垣内
kamado 竈
kami 神
kannō 勧農
karamushi
katei 課丁
kebiishi chō 検非違使庁
keichō 計帳
kensha 験者
kieki 飢疫
ko 戸
koeki (labor) 雇役
kōeki (trade) 交易
kokufu 国府
Kōnin shiki 弘仁式
Konjaku monogatari shū 今昔物語集
ko-ryō 戸令
koseki 戸籍

kubunden 区分田

kuso kōji 糞小路

kyaku 格

kyū kyū ritsuryō no gotoshi
急急如律令

mafu 麻布

majinai まじない

maki 巻

Man'yōshū 万葉集

mappō jidai 末法時代

mokei kamado 模型竃

mukotori kon 婿取り婚

munashiki ko no yamai 空き子の病い

myō 名

Naimushō chiri kyoku 内務省地理局

Nihon chūsei kaihatsu shi no kenkyū
日本開発史の研究

Nihon kiryaku 日本紀略

Nihon nisen nen no jinkō shi
日本二千年の人口史

Nihon sandai jitsuroku 日本三代実録

Nihon shippei shi 日本疾病史

Nijō-ōji 二条大路

noroi 呪い

nuhi 奴婢

ōchō kokka 王朝国家

ōgaki 大垣

ōharae 大祓え

onna bori 女堀り

ōnendai ki 大年代記

onryō 怨霊

rajō 羅城

riben zhuan 日本伝

rikiden no yakara 力田の輩

rikkoku shi 六国史

rinji zōyaku 臨時雑役

Rissho zanpen 律書残編

ritsuryō 律令

Saikyūki 西宮記

sato dairi 里内裏

seitei 正丁

shibu shitaji 渋下地

shichō 仕丁

shiohama 塩浜

shiotsutsumi 塩堤

shishō zu 四証図

shōen 荘園

shōen-kokugaryō 荘園国衙領

shoki shōen 初期荘園

Shoku Nihongi 続日本紀

Shūgai shō 拾芥抄

shugen dō 修験道

shūri shiki 修理職

sōtaiteki dorei sei 総体的奴隷制

Sung shu 宋書

taima 大麻

tan 段

tatara たたら 踏鞴

tateana jūkyo 竪穴住居

tato 田堵

tenka 天下

tennō 天皇

tokusei 徳政

tsuku no hitobito 客作児

urushi shitaji 漆下地

Wamyō shō 和名抄

Yamai no sōshi 病草紙

za 座

zōyō 雑徭

zuryō 受領

BIBLIOGRAPHY

The place of publication is not listed for those works printed in Tokyo.

ABBREVIATIONS

NKBT   *Nihon koten bungaku taikei*
NST   *Nihon shisō taikei*
SZKT   *Shintei zōho kokushi taikei*

PRIMARY SOURCES

Chūgoku seishi Nihon den 2 Jiu Tang shu Wo guo riben zhuan. Sung shu riben zhuan. Yuan shi riben zhuan. Edited by Ishihara Michihiro. Iwanami bunko, 1986.

Chūyūki. Zōho shiryō taisei, vols. 9-15. Kyoto: Rinsen shoten, 1965.

Eishō ki. Zōho shiryō taisei, vol. 8. Kyoto: Rinsen shoten, 1965.

Engi shiki. SZKT, vol. 26. Yoshikawa kōbunkan, 1977.

Hara chō karyoku hatsuden sho kanren iseki chōsa hōkoku 1, 3, 5, 7, 8. Fukushima-shi: Fukushima-ken kyōiku iinkai, 1990, 1992, 1995, and 1998, respectively.

Heian ibun. 13 vols. Edited by Takeuchi Rizō. Tokyo dō, 1965.

Honchō seiki. SZKT, vol. 9. Yoshikawa kōbunkan, 1964.

Hyakuren shō. SZKT, vol. 11. Yoshikawa kōbunkan, 1929.

Kanoko C iseki urushigami monjo: honbun hen. Ibaraki-ken: Ibaraki-ken kyōiku zaidan, 1983.

Kinsei Iriki monjo. Edited by Abe Yoshio et al. Tokyo daigaku shuppan kai, 1981.

Kōnin shiki. SZKT, vol. 26. Yoshikawa kōbunkan, 1937.

Konjaku monogatari shū. NKBT, vols. 22-27. Edited by Yamada Takao et al. Iwanami shoten, 1961.

Miyoshi Kiyoyuki. *Iken jūnikajō.* NST, vol. 8, *Kodai seiji shakai shisō,* edited by Takeuchi Rizō et al., 75-101. Iwanami shoten, 1979.

Nihon kiryaku. SZKT, vols. 10-11. Yoshikawa kōbunkan, 1929.

Nihon sandai jitsuroku. SZKT, vol. 4. Yoshikawa kōbunkan, 1934.

Nihon shoki. NKBT, vols. 67-68. Edited by Sakamoto Tarō et al. Iwanami shoten, 1965.

Nōrin gyō: Chōki keizai tōkei. Vol.9. Tōyō keizai shinpō sha, 1966.

Onnabori: Chūsei shoki nōgyō yōsui shi hakkutsu chōsa. Gunma: Gunma-ken maizō bunka zai chōsa jigyō dan, 1984.

Owari no kuni gebumi. NST, vol. 8, *Kodai seiji shakai shisō,* edited by Takeuchi Rizō et al., 253-68. Iwanami shoten, 1979.

Rissho zanpen 27 Kaitei shiseki shūran. Shiseki shūran kenkyū kai, 1969.

Ritsuryō. NST, vol. 3. Iwanami shoten, 1975.

Ruijū fusen shō. SZKT, vol. 27. Yoshikawa kōbunkan, 1933.

Ruijū sandai kyaku SZKT, vol. 25. Yoshikawa kōbunkan, 1936.

Ryō no shūge. SZKT, vols. 23-24. Yoshikawa kōbunkan, 1966.

Saikyūki 6 Kojitsu sōsho. Vol. 1. Meiji tosho shuppan, 1993.

Shin sarugakki. NST, vol. 8, *Kodai seiji shakai shisō,* edited by Takeuchi Rizō et al., 133-52. Iwanami shoten, 1979.

Shohon shūsei Wamyō ruijū shō: Honbun hen. Kyoto: Rinsen shoten, 1968.

Shoku Nihongi. SZKT, vol. 2. Yoshikawa kōbunkan, 1935.

Shūgai shō 22 Kojitsu sōsho. Meiji tosho shuppan, 1993.

Sōma kaihatsu kanren iseki chōsa hōkoku 1: Honbun 1, 2. Fukushima-shi: Fukushima-ken kyōiku iinkai, 1989 and 1991, respectively.

Takatsuki shi shi: Kōko hen. Takatsuki-shi: Takatsuki-shi, 1973.

Utsubo monogatari. NKBT, vols. 10-12. Iwanami shoten, 1959-62.

Wamyō ruijū shō gun gō ri eki mei kōshō. Edited by Ikebe Wataru. Yoshikawa kōbunkan, 1981.

Yamai no sōshi. In *Nihon no emaki,* vol. 7, edited by Komatsu Shigemi. Chūo kōron sha, 1987.

SECONDARY SOURCES

Adolphson, Mikael S. *The Gates of Power: Monks, Courtiers, and Warriors in Pre-Modern Japan.* Honolulu: University of Hawai'i Press, 2000.

Amino Yoshihiko. *Chūsei minshū no seigyō to gijutsu.* Tokyo daigaku shuppan kai, 2001.

———. "Chūsei no futan taikei--nengu ni tsuite." In *Chūsei kinsei no kokka to shakai,* edited by Nagahara Keiji et al., 72-103. Tokyo daigaku shuppan kai, 1986.

———. *Nihon chūsei no hinōgyōmin to tennō.* Iwanami shoten, 1984.

———. *Nihon chūsei no minshū zō.* Iwanami shoten, 1980.

Aoki Kazuo. "Koeki sei no seiritsu." *Shigaku zasshi* 67 (April 1958): 1-30.

Asaka Toshiki. "Kodai no Hokuriku dō ni okeru kanshin shinkō." *Nihon kai bunka* 6 (March 1979): 1-29.

Barnes, Gina. "Review of *Sacred Texts and Buried Treasures: Issues in the Historical Archaeology of Ancient Japan*," *Monumenta Nipponica* 54 (spring 1999): 124-27.

———. *Protohistoric Yamato*. Ann Arbor: University of Michigan Press, 1988.

Barnes, Gina, and Masaaki Okita. "Japanese Archaeology in the 1990s." *Journal of Archaeological Research* 7 (1999): 349-95.

Breen, John, and Mark Teeuwen, eds. *Shinto in History: Ways of the Kami*. Honolulu: University of Hawai'i Press, 2000.

Brown, Philip C. *Central Authority and Local Autonomy in the Formation of Early Modern Japan*. Stanford: Stanford University Press, 1993.

———. "The Mismeasure of Land: Land Surveying in the Tokugawa Period." *Monumenta Nipponica* 42 (summer 1987): 115-55.

Cavanaugh, Carole. "Text and Textile: Unweaving the Female Subject in Heian Writing." *Positions* 4 (winter 1996): 595-636.

Coale, Ansley, and Paul Demeny. *Regional Model Life Tables and Stable Populations*. Princeton: Princeton University Press, 1966.

Emori Itsuo. "Kon'in keitai to shūzoku." In *Nihon no kodai* 11 *Uji to ie*, edited by Ōbayashi Taryō, 111-58. Chūō kōron sha, 1987.

Engi-shiki: Procedures of the Engi Era. Translated by Felicia Bock. Sophia University, 1970.

Farris, William Wayne. "Pieces in a Puzzle: The History of the Shōsōin Documents." *Monumenta Nipponica* 62 (winter) 2008: 1-40

———. "Famine, Climate, and Farming in Early Japan, 670-1100." In *Heian Japan, Centers and Peripheries*, edited by Mikael Adolphson, Edward Kamens, and Stacie Matsumoto, 275-304. Honolulu: University of Hawai'i Press, 2007.

———. *Japan's Medieval Population: Famine, Fertility, and Warfare in a Transformative Age*. Honolulu: University of Hawai'i Press, 2006.

———. *Sacred Texts and Buried Treasures: Issues in the Historical Archaeology of Ancient Japan*. Honolulu: University of Hawai'i Press, 1998.

———. "Diseases of the Premodern Period in Japan." In *The Cambridge World History of Human Disease*, edited by Kenneth F. Kiple, 376-85. Cambridge: Cambridge University Press, 1993.

———. *Heavenly Warriors: The Evolution of Japan's Military, 500-1300*. Council on East Asian Studies, Harvard University, 1992.

———. *Population, Disease, and Land in Early Japan, 645-900*. Council on East Asian Studies, Harvard University, 1985.

Fox, Robin. *Kinship and Marriage*. Harmondsworth: Penguin Books, 1967.

Friday Karl. *Samurai, Warfare and the State in Early Medieval Japan*. New York and London: Routledge Press, 2004.

————. "Pushing Beyond the Pale: The Yamato Conquest of the *Emishi* and Northern Japan." *Journal of Japanese Studies* 23 (winter 1997): 1-24.

————. *Hired Swords: The Rise of Private Warrior Power in Early Japan.* Stanford: Stanford University Press, 1992.

Fujikawa Yū. *Nihon shippei shi.* Heibon sha, 1969.

Fukuhara Eitarō. "Futatabi Tenpyō kyūnen no ekibyō ryūkō to sono eikyō ni tsuite." In *Kankyō rekishigaku no shiza,* edited by Hashimoto Masayoshi, 75-106. Iwata shoin, 2002.

————. "Tenpyō kyūnen no ekibyō ryūkō to sono seijiteki eikyō ni tsuite." *Kōbe Yamate daigaku kankyō bunka kenkyū jo kiyō* 4 (2000): 27-39.

Furushima Toshio. *Furushima Toshio chosaku shū 6 Nihon nōgyō gijutsu shi.* Tokyo daigaku shuppan kai, 1975.

Gomi Fumihiko. *Insei ki shakai no kenkyū.* Yamakawa shuppan sha, 1984.

Gomi Fumihiko, and Watanabe Hisashi, eds., *Shin taikei Nihon shi 3 Tochi shoyū shi.* Yamakawa shuppan, 2002.

Gotō Tadatoshi. "Ro no kōzō ni tsuite." In *Kodai Nihon no tetsu to shakai,* 109-17. Heibon sha, 1982.

Gottfried, Robert. *The Black Death.* New York: The Free Press, 1983.

Grapard, Alan. "Religious Practices." In Vol. 2, *The Cambridge History of Japan,* edited by Donald H. Shively and William McCullough, 517-75. Cambridge: Cambridge University Press, 1999.

Groner, Paul. *Ryōgen and Mount Hiei.* Honolulu: University of Hawai'i Press, 2002.

————. *Saichō: The Establishment of the Japanese Tendai School.* Buddhist Studies Series. Berkeley: Asian Humanities Press, 1985.

Habu, Junko. *Ancient Jomon of Japan.* Cambridge: Cambridge University Press, 2004.

Hakeda, Yoshito. *Kukai: Major Works.* New York: Columbia University Press, 1972.

Hall, John. *Government and Local Power in Japan, 500-1700.* Princeton: Princeton University Press, 1966.

Hall, Kenneth. "Economic History of Early Southeast Asia." In *The Cambridge History of Southeast Asia,* edited by Nicholas Tarling, 1:183-275. Cambridge: Cambridge University Press, 1992.

Hanihara Kazurō. "Estimation of the Number of Early Migrants to Japan: A Simulative Study." *Journal of the Anthropological Society of Nippon* 95 (July 1987): 391-403.

Hanley, Susan. *Everyday Things in Premodern Japan.* Berkeley: University of California Press, 1997.

Harada Nobuo. *Chūsei sonraku no keikan to seikatsu.* Kyoto: Shibunkaku, 1999.

Harashima Reiji. "Hasseiki no inasaku ni kansuru ni san no mondai." *Rekishi hyōron* 148 (December 1962): 24-39.

Hatai Hiromu. "Nara Heian jidai no yakibata nōgyō." In *Chūsei shakai no seiritsu to tenkai*, 1-140. Yoshikawa kōbunkan, 1976.

Hattori Toshirō. *Heian jidai igaku no kenkyū.* Kuwana bunsei dō, 1955.

Hayakawa Shōhachi. *Nihon no rekishi 3 Ritsuryō kokka.* Shōgakkan, 1974.

―――. "Ritsuryō zaisei no kōzō to sono henshitsu." In *Nihon keizai shi taikei 1 Kodai*, edited by Iyanaga Teizō, 259-80. Tokyo daigaku shuppan kai, 1965.

―――. "Hihyō to shōkai." *Shigaku zasshi* 71 (August 1962): 74-101.

Hayami Akira. "The Population at the Beginning of the Tokugawa Period--An Introduction to the Historical Demography of Pre-Industrial Japan." *Keio Economic Studies* 4 (1966): 1-28.

Hayami Akira, and Miyamoto Matao. "Gaisetsu: Jūnana jūhasseiki." In *Nihon keizai shi 1 Keizai shakai no seiritsu jūnana jūhasseiki,* edited by Hayami Akira and Miyamoto Matao, 4-84. Iwanami shoten 1988.

Hayashi Hiromichi. "Kamado shutsugen ni kansuru ni san mondai." In *Mizu to tsuchi no kōkogaku,* 95-110. Jōyō-shi: Kōyū kai, 1973.

"Heijō-kyō no rajō, kanryaku ban ka." *Asahi shinbun,* March 15, 2006.

Hirai Kiyoshi. *Zusetsu Nihon jūtaku no rekishi.* Gakugei shuppan sha, 1980.

―――. *Nihon jūtaku no rekishi.* NHK bukkusu, 1974.

Hotate Michihisa. "Chūsei minshū keizai no tenkai." In *Kōza Nihon rekishi 3 Chūsei 1,* 167-206. Tokyo daigaku shuppan kai, 1984.

Hudson, Mark. *Ruins of Identity: Ethnogenesis in the Japanese Islands.* Honolulu: University of Hawai'i Press, 1999.

Ihara Kesao. "Shohyō." *Shakai keizai shigaku* 60 (September 1994): 84-88.

Imazu Katsunori. "Nihon kodai no sonraku to chiiki shakai." *Kōkogaku kenkyū* 50 (December 2003): 57-74.

―――. "Taihō ninen Mino no kuni Kamo no kohori Hanyū no sato koseki o megutte." In *Okayama daigaku gakunai kyōdō kenkyū 'shizen to ningen no kyōsei' hokukusho: Bungaku bu sabute-ma: 'Kankyō' to bunka bunmei rekishi,* 23-33. Okayama: Okayama daigaku, 2003.

Inagaki Yasuhiko. "Chūsei no nōgyō keiei to shūshu keitai." In *Iwanami kōza Nihon rekishi 6 Chūsei 2,* 167-205. Iwanami shoten, 1975.

―――. "Shoki myōden no kōzō." In *Chūsei no shakai to keizai,* edited by Inagaki Yasuhiko and Nagahara Keiji, 1-80. Tokyo daigaku shuppan kai, 1962.

Inaki Yoshikazu. "'Wayō' bijutsu to Heian jidai no shūkyō kan." *Nihon shūkyō bunka shi kenkyū* 6.1 (2002): 31-45.

Inoue Masao. "Heian chūki no dōsen ryūtsū tozetsu to shichō kenryoku kakujū no mondai." *Shakai keizai shigaku* 66 (March 2000): 3-22.

Inoue Tatsuo. "Ko-ryō ōbun jō no seiritsu." In *Nihon kodai shi ronshū*, 2:129-76. Yoshikawa kōbunkan, 1962.

Irumada Nobuo, and Tomiyama Kazuyuki. *Kita no Hiraizumi, minami no Ryukyu*. Chūō kōron sha, 2002.

Ishii Kenji. *Nihon no fune*. Sōgen sha, 1957.

Ishii Susumu. *Nihon no chūsei 1 Chūsei no katachi*. Chūō kōron sha, 2002.

———. *Kamakura bushi no jitsuzō*. Heibon sha, 1987.

Ishimoda Shō. *Nihon no kodai kokka*. Iwanami shoten, 1971.

Isogai Fujio. *Chūsei no nōgyō to kikō*. Yoshikawa kōbunkan, 2002.

———. "Nihon chūsei shi kenkyū to kikō hendō ron." *Nihon shi kenkyū* 388 (December 1994): 25-49.

———. "Shohyō." *Rekishi hyōron* 524 (December 1993): 97-102.

Isogawa Shin'ya. "Kodai chūsei no chūtetsu imono." *Kokuritsu rekishi minzoku hakubutsukan kenkyū kiyō* 46 (December 1992): 1-80.

Itō Toshikazu. "Heian Kamakura jidai no yakibata ni kansuru rekishi chirigakuteki kenkyū." *Nihon joshi daigaku bungaku bu kiyō* 45 (1995): 79-96.

Itō Toshio. *Mono to ningen no bunka shi 68-I Kinu*. Hōsei daigaku shuppan kyoku, 1992.

Iwaki Takatoshi. "Goryō-e no hassei." In *Kokushi ronshū*, 1:443-58. Dokushi kai, 1959.

Iyanaga Teizō. *Nihon kodai shakai keizai shi kenkyū*. Iwanami shoten, 1980.

———. *Zusetsu Nihon no rekishi 5 kizoku to bushi*. Iwanami shoten, 1980.

———. *Nara jidai no kizoku to nōmin*. Jibun dō, 1956.

Izumi Takeshi. "Ritsuryō saishi ron ichi shiten." In *Dōkyō to higashi Ajia*, edited by Fukunaga Mitsuji, 55-99. Jinbun shoin, 1989.

Jannetta, Ann. *Epidemics and Mortality in Early Modern Japan*. Princeton: Princeton University Press, 1987.

———. "Review Essay: Historical Demography in East Asia." *Journal of Family History* 11 (winter 1986): 384-86.

Kagetsu Yōichirō. "Teijū." In *Nihon minzoku bunka taikei 6 Hyōhaku to teichaku*, 431-62. Shōgakkan, 1984.

Kagose Yoshiaki. *Teishitchi*. Kokin shoin, 1972.

Kamata Motokazu. "Nihon kodai no jinkō ni tsuite." *Mokkan kenkyū* 6 (1984): 131-54.

Kamei Meitoku. "NisSō bōeki no tenkai." In *Iwanami kōza Nihon tsūshi 6 Kodai 5*, 112-38. Iwanami shoten, 1993.

Kaneko Hiroyuki. "Nihon ni okeru hitogata no kigen." In *Dōkyō to higashi Ajia*, edited by Fukunaga Mitsuji, 37-54. Jinbun shoin, 1989.

———, ed. *Ritsuryō ki saishi ibutsu shūsei*. Nara kokuritsu bunka zai kenkyū jo, 1988.

———. "Tojō to saishi." In *Okinoshima to kodai saishi*, edited by Oda Fujio,

198-226. Yoshikawa kōbunkan, 1988.

―――. "Tojin no seishin seikatsu." In *Nihon no kodai 9 Tōjō no seitai*, edited by Kishi Toshio, 319-64. Chūō kōron sha, 1987.

―――. "Heijō kyō to saijō." *Kokuritsu rekishi minzoku hakubutsukan kenkyū hōkoku 7* (March 1985): 219-90.

―――, ed. "Saishi kankei ibutsu shutsudo chi chimei hyō." *Kokuritsu rekishi minzoku hakubutsukan kenkyū hōkoku fuhen 7* (March 1985): 1-805.

―――. "Mokusei mozōhin." In *Shintō kōkogaku kōza*, 3:69-88. Yūzan kaku, 1981.

―――. "Kodai no mokusei mozō hin." *Nara kokuritsu bunka zai kenkyū jo kenkyū ronshū 6* (March 1980): 5-28.

Kanō Hisashi, and Kinoshita Masashi. "Shio tetsu no seisan to kōnō." In *Kodai no chihō shi 2 San'in nankai hen*, edited by Yagi Atsuru, 172-206. Asakura shoten, 1977.

Katō Sadako. "Kyakusaku jiyaku no shiteki igi." *Kodai bunka 27* (February 1975): 32-46.

Kawane Yoshihira. "Shohyō to shokai." *Nihon rekishi 556* (September 1994): 113-15.

―――. "Izumi Kōnō ke monjo chū no Heian makki no monjo ni tsuite." *Ritsumeikan bungaku 521* (June 1991): 120-25.

Keirstead, Thomas. *The Geography of Power in Medieval Japan*. Princeton: Princeton University Press, 1992.

Kiley, Cornelius. "Provincial Administration and Land Tenure in Early Heian." In Vol. 2, *The Cambridge History of Japan*, edited by Donald H. Shively and William McCullough, 236-340. Cambridge: Cambridge University Press, 1999.

Kimura Shigemitsu. *Hatake to Nihonjin*. Chūkō shinsho, 1996.

―――. "Kenkyū nooto." *Jinmin no rekishigaku 126* (January 1996): 30-36.

―――. *Nihon kodai chūsei hatasaku shi no kenkyū*. Azekura shobo, 1992.

―――. "Chūsei zenki no nōgyō seisanryoku to hatasaku." *Nihon shi kenkyū 280* (December 1985): 52-82.

―――. "Dai kaikon jidai no kaihatsu." In *Gijutsu no shakai shi 1 Kodai chūsei no gijutsu to shakai*, edited by Miura Keiichi, 150-204. Yuhikaku, 1982.

Kinda Akihiro. *Bichikei to chūsei sonraku*. Yoshikawa kōbunkan, 1993.

―――. *Kodai Nihon no keikan*. Yoshikawa kōbunkan, 1993.

―――. "Kokuzu no jōri puran to shōen no jōri puran." *Nihonshi kenkyū 332* (April 1990): 1-35.

―――. *Jōri to sonraku no rekishi chirigaku kenkyū*. Daimei dō, 1985.

Kishi Toshio. *Kodai kyūto no tankyū*. Hanawa shobō, 1984.

―――. *Nihon kodai sekichō no kenkyū*. Hanawa shobō, 1973.

Kitō Hiroshi. *Jinkō kara yomu Nihon no rekishi*. Kōdan sha, 2000.

————. "'Chōsa' Meiji izen Nihon chiiki jinkō." *Jōchi keizai ronshū* 41 (March 1996): 65-79.

————. *Edo jidai no jinkō to shakai.* Jōchi daigaku, 1990.

————. *Nihon nisen nen no jinkō shi.* PHP Paperbacks, 1983.

Kobayashi Kazumasa. "Jinkō jinruigaku." In *Jinruigaku kōza* 11 *Jinkō,* edited by Kobayashi Kazumasa, 63-130. Yūzan kaku, 1979.

Kōchi Shōsuke. "Taihō-ryō handen shūju seido kō." *Shigaku zasshi* 86 (March 1977): 1-39.

"Kokufu kenkyū no genjō--sono ni." *Kokuritsu rekishi minzoku hakubutsukan kenkyū hōkoku* 20 (March 1989): 278-384.

Kōmoto Masayuki. "Yayoi jidai no shakai." In *Kodai shi hakkutsu* 4 *Inasaku no hajimari,* edited by Sahara Makoto and Kanaseki Hiroshi. Kōdan sha, 1975.

Kondō Ariyoshi. "Hōryūji tōin no Kuse Kannon zō anchi ni tsuite." *Nihon rekishi* 653 (October 2002): 1-17.

Kōno Michiaki. *Nihon nōkō gu shi no kisoteki kenkyū.* Izumi shoin, 1994.

Koyama Shūzō. *Jōmon jidai.* Chūō kōron, 1984.

————. "Jōmon Subsistence and Population." *Senri Ethnological Studies* 2 (1978): 1-65.

Kuroda Hideo. *Nihon chūsei kaihatsu shi no kenkyū.* Azekura shobō, 1984.

————. "Chūsei no kaihatsu to shizen." In *Ikki* 4 *Seikatsu bunka shisō,* 91-130. Tokyo daigaku shuppan kai, 1981.

Kushiki Yoshinori. "Nagaya ōke no shōhi to ryūtsū keizai." *Kokuritsu rekishi minzoku hakubutsu kan kenkyū hōkoku* 92 (February 2002): 7-34.

————. "Shōnin to shōgyō no hassei." In *Shin taikei Nihon shi* 12 *Ryūtsū keizai shi,* 81-111. Yamakawa shuppan sha, 2002.

————. "Kokuga chōhatsu rikieki no kōzō to hensen." In *Nihon no zenkindai to Hokuriku shakai,* 101-32. Kyoto: Shibunkaku, 1989.

————. "Heian jidai Kyoto ni okeru rikieki." *Hisutoria* 108 (September 1985): 1-16.

McCullough, William. "The Capital and Its Society." In Vol. 2, *The Cambridge History of Japan,* edited by Donald H. Shively and William McCullough, 97-182. Cambridge: Cambridge University Press, 1999.

————. "The Heian Court, 794-1070." In Vol. 2, *The Cambridge History of Japan,* edited by Donald H. Shively and William McCullough, 20-96. Cambridge: Cambridge University Press, 1999.

————. "Japanese Marital institutions in the Heian period." *Harvard Journal of Asiatic Studies* 27 (1967): 103-67.

McMullin, Neil. "On Placating the Gods and Pacifying the Populace: The Case of the Gion *Goryo* Cult." *History of Religions* 27 (February 1988): 270-93.

McNeill, William. *Plagues and Peoples.* New York: Doubleday, 1976.

Maeda Ryōichi. "'Kyūkyū ritsuryō no gotoshi' o saguru." In *Dōkyō to higashi Ajia*, edited by Fukunaga Mitsuji, 101-26. Jinbun shoin, 1989.

Maeda Tetsushi. "Harima no kuni Akaho gun Hisatomi ho no kihon shiryō ni tsuite." *Matsukaneyama ronsō* 30 (1996) 31-54.

Maruyama Hitoshi. "Insei ki ni okeru goganji zōei jigyō." *Nenpō chūsei shi kenkyū* 26 (2001): 85-112.

Maruyama Yoshihiko. *Kodai Tōdaiji shōen no kenkyū*. Keisui sha, 2001.

Maruyama Yumiko. "Kodai no tennō to byōsha." In *Iwanami kōza Tennō to ōken o kangaeru 8 Kosumorojii to shintai*, 203-26. Iwanami shoten, 2002.

———. *Tenpyō no hikari to kage*. Nihon hōsō shuppan kyokai, 1999.

Matsubara Hironobu. "Shūrishiki ni tsuite no ichi kenkyū." *Hisutoria* 78 (March 1978): 1-22.

Matsumae Takeshi. "Gion gozu ten'ō sha no sōken to tennō shinkō no genryū." In *Kodai gaku sōron*, 435-46. Tsunoda Bun'ei sensei koki kinen jigyō kai, 1983.

Meiji zen Nihon sangyō gijutsu shi. Nihon gakujutsu shinkō kai, 1960.

Mesner, Thomas. "Lamp oil, Miso, and Moss: The Variety of Estate Revenues in the Heian Period." *Journal of Intercultural Studies* 20 (1993): 14-24.

Minegishi Sumio. *Chūsei saigai senran no shakai shi*. Yoshikawa kōbunkan, 2001.

———. "Onnabori." In *Tōsonshi*, 212-19. Gendai shobō shinsha, 1979.

Miraculous Tales of the Lotus Sutra From Ancient Japan. Translated by Yoshiko Dykstra. Osaka: Kansai University of Foreign Studies, 1983.

Miskimin, Harry. *The Economy of Early Renaissance Europe, 1300-1460*. Cambridge: Cambridge University Press, 1975.

Miyamoto Tasuku. "Nihon kodai kazoku hō no shiteki ichikōsatsu." *Kodai gaku* 3 (December 1954): 366-84.

Miyataki Kōji. "'Saga-chō' ki ni okeru tōgoku shūraku no saikentō." *Kodai bunka* 54 (November 2002): 19-26.

Mizuno Masayoshi. "Uma-uma-uma: sono katari no kōkogaku." *Bunka zai gakuhō* 2 (March 1983): 23-43.

Mizuno Shōji. *Nihon chūsei no sonraku to shōen sei*. Azekura shobō, 2000.

Mochida Yasuhiko. "Nara chō kizoku no ninzu henka ni tsuite." *Gakushūin shigaku* 15 (January 1979): 17-35.

Mori Kōzō. "Ōzone iseki." *Mokkan kenkyū* 12 (1990): 86.

Moriyama Shigeki, and Nakae Kazue. *Nihon kodomo shi*. Heibon sha, 2002.

Morris, Dana. "Land and Society." In Vol. 2, *The Cambridge History of Japan*, edited by Donald Shively and William McCullough, 183-235. Cambridge: Cambridge University Press, 1999.

———. "Peasant Economy in Early Japan, 650-950." PhD diss., University of California at Berkeley, 1980.

Murao Jirō. *Ritsuryō zaisei shi no kenkyū*. Yoshikawa kōbunkan, 1961.

Naga Yōichi. "Jōgan gonen goryō e ni tsuite no ichi shiron." *Kyushu shigaku* 5 (August 1957): 17-26.

Nagahara Keiji. "Chūsei kinsei ikōki no gijutsu seisanryoku no hatten." In *Kokushigaku ronshū*, 231-52. Imai Rintarō sensei kijū kinen ronbun shū kankō kai, 1988.

———. *Nihon no chūsei shakai*. Iwanami shoten, 1968.

Nagasawa Hiroshi. "Chūseiteki jimoku toshite no hata no seiritsu." *Shigaku kenkyū* 152 (June 1981): 1-22.

Nakamura, James. "Human Capital Accumulation in Premodern Rural Japan." *The Journal of Economic History* 41 (June 1981): 263-81.

Nakao Yoshiharu. *Kōkogaku no raiburari-, 46 Naniwa no miyako*. Nyū saiensu sha, 1986.

Nakata Kaoru. "Yōrō ko-ryō ōbun jō no kenkyū." In Vol. 1, *Hōsei shi ronshū*, 43-83. Iwanami shoten, 1926.

Naumann, Nelly. "The State Cult of the Nara and Early Heian Periods." In *Shinto in History: Ways of the Kami,* edited by John Breen and Mark Teeuwen, 53-62. Honolulu: University of Hawai'i Press, 2000.

Nihon kodai no tetsu seisan. Rokkō shuppan, 1991.

Nihongi: Chronicles of Japan from the Earliest Times to A.D. 697. Translated by Willam Aston. London: Kegan, Trench, and Trubner, 1896.

Nishimura Hiroko. *Kodai chūsei kazoku to josei*. Yoshikawa kōbunkan, 2002.

———. "*Konjaku monogatari* ni okeru kon'in keitai to kon'in kankei." *Rekishi hyōron* 335 (March 1978): 39-53.

Nishimura Makoto, and Yoshikawa Ichirō, eds. *Nihon kyōkō shi kō*. Maruzen, 1936.

Nishio Masato. "Ekibyō kami shinkō no seiritsu." In *Minzoku shūkyō 3 Ōken to shamanizumu*, 255-80. Tokyo dō, 1990.

Nishitani Tadashi. "Kara chiiki to hokubu Kyushu." In Vol. 1, *Dazaifu ko bunka ronsō*, 36-46. Yoshikawa kōbunkan, 1983.

Nishiyachi Seibi. "Kajishi to suiko." In *Iwanami kōza Nihon tsūshi 7 Chūsei 1*, 313-28. Iwanami shoten, 1993.

———. "Chūsei seiritsu ki ni okeru kajishi no seikaku." *Nihon shi kenkyū* 275 (July 1985): 1-25.

Nishiyama Ryōhei. "Goryō shinkō ron." In *Iwanami kōza Nihon tsūshi 5 Kodai 4*, 333-46. Iwanami shoten, 1993.

Ogata Tetsushi. "Nijō ōji mokkan no jumon." *Mokkan kenkyū* 18 (1996): 246.

Ogawa Makoto. *Chūsei toshi 'fuchū' no tenkai*. Shibunkaku, 2001.

Ōhashi Shin'ya. "Biwa ko ni ikiru." In *Kankyō rekishigaku no shiza*, edited by Hashimoto Yoshimasa, 35-73. Iwata shoin 2002.

Okuno Nakahiko. "Rinji zōyaku no seiritsu to tenkai." *Nihon rekishi* 255

(August 1969): 32-49.

Ōmachi Ken. "Nihon kodai no furō seisaku ni okeru shozaichishugi to futatsu no honganchishugi." *Nihonshi kenkyū* 486 (February 2003): 1-26.

Ono Masatoshi. *Zukai Nihon no chūsei iseki.* Tokyo daigaku shuppan kai, 2001.

Ōno Tsutomu. "Heian jidai no goryō shisō." *Nihon rekishi* 114 (December 1957): 41-49.

Ōshima Tatehiko. *Ekishin to sono shūhen.* Iwasaki bijutsu sha, 1985.

Ōtsu Tōru. *Ritsuryō kokka shihai kōzō no kenkyū.* Iwanami shoten, 1993.

Piggott, Joan. "Sacral Kingship and Confederacy in Early Izumo." *Monumenta Nipponica* 44 (spring 1989): 45-74.

Rambelli, Fabio, and Mark Teeuwen, eds. *Buddhas and Kami in Japan.* London: Routledge Curzon, 2003.

Reischauer, Edwin O., John Fairbank, and Albert Craig. *East Asia: Tradition and Transformation.* Boston: Houghton Mifflin, 1989.

Saeki Arikiyo. *Nihon kodai no seiji to shakai.* Yoshikawa kōbunkan, 1970.

Saitō Osamu. "The Frequency of Famines as Demographic Correctives in the Japanese Past." *The Institute of Economic Research, Hitotsubashi University: Discussion Paper Series A* 386 (January 2000): 1-32.

———. "Inasaku to hatten no hikaku shi." In *Tōnan Ajia kara no chiteki bōken,* 195-240. Libro, 1986.

Sakaguchi Toshiyuki, "Magarigawa iseki." *Mokkan kenkyū* 9 (1987): 29.

Sakamoto Shōzō. *Nihon no rekishi 6 Sekkan jidai.* Shōgakkan, 1974.

———. *Nihon ōchō kokka taisei ron.* Tokyo daigaku shuppan kai, 1972.

Sakamoto Tarō. *Sakamoto Tarō chosaku shū 7 Ritsuryō seido.* Yoshikawa kōbunkan, 1989.

Sakaue Yasutoshi. "Nara Heian jidai jinkō deeta no saikentō." *Nihonshi kenkyū* 536 (April 2007): 1-18.

Sakō Nobuyuki. "Ekishin shinkō no seiritsu." In *Mura kōzō to takai kan,* 113-36. Yūzan kaku, 1985.

Sansom, George. *A History of Japan to 1334.* Stanford: Stanford University Press, 1958.

Sasaki Gin'ya. "Sangyō no bunka to chūsei shōgyō." In *Nihon keizai shi taikei 2 Chūsei,* edited by Nagahara Keiji, 143-88. Tokyo daigaku shuppan kai, 1965.

Sasaki Junnosuke, ed.. *Nihon chūsei kōki kinsei shoki ni okeru kikin to sensō no kenkyū.* Waseda daigaku kyōiku gakubu, 2000.

Satō Yasuhiro. *Nihon chūsei no rinmei.* Kyoto daigaku gakujutsu shuppan kai, 2001.

———. "Heian jidai no kuni no kendan." *Shirin* 75 (September 1991): 33-68.

Sawada Goichi. *Nara chō jidai minsei keizai no sūteki kenkyū.* Kashiwa shobō, 1972.

Sekiguchi Hiroko. "Nihon kodai ni okeru fūfu gōsō no ippanteki fuzai." *Seisen joshi daigaku jinbun kagaku kenkyū kiyō* 22 (2001): 147-90.

———. *Nihon kodai kon'in shi no kenkyū*. 2 vols. Hanawa shobō, 1993.

Sekiguchi Yasuyuki. "Ekishin saishi chi to shūyō kōtsū ro." *Chiri gakuhō* 28 (1992): 111-28.

Sekine Masataka. *Nara chō shoku seikatsu no kenkyū*. Yoshikawa kōbunkan, 1969.

Serizawa Chōsuke. *Sekki jidai no Nihon*. Tsukiji shokan, 1960.

Shibata Minoru. *Goryō shinkō*. Yūzan kaku, 1984.

Shiraishi Taichirō. "Chūsei yōgyō no rinmei." In *Kōza Nihon gijutsu no shakai shi* 4 *Yōgyō*, 91-118. Nihon hyōron sha, 1984.

Smith, Thomas. *The Agrarian Origins of Modern Japan*. Stanford: Stanford University Press, 1959.

Sonoda Kōyū. "Suiko: Tenpyō kara Engi made." In *Ritsuryō kokka no kiso kōzō*, 397-466. Yoshikawa kōbunkan, 1960.

Sumi Tōyō. *Zenkindai Nihon kazoku no kōzō*. Kōbun dō, 1983.

Suzuki Tetsuo. *Chūsei Nihon no kaihatsu to hyakusei*. Iwata shoin, 2001.

———. "Shohyō." *Shikai* 36 (June 1993): 78-83.

———. "Echigo no kuni Ishii no shō ni okeru 'kaihatsu' to rōnin." *Nihonshi kenkyū* 303 (November 1987): 30-47.

Taeuber, Irene. *The Population of Japan*. Princeton: Princeton University Press, 1958.

Takahashi Bonsen. *Nihon jinkō shi no kenkyū*. Vol.1. San'yū sha, 1941.

Takahashi Manabu. "Kodai matsu ikō ni okeru chikei kankyō no henbō to tochi kaihatsu." *Nihonshi kenkyū* 380 (April 1994): 33-49.

Takahashi Takashi. "Shohyō." *Rekishigaku kenkyū* 655 (February 1994): 43-45.

———. "Yogore no Kyoto, goryō e, bushi." *Atarashii rekishigaku no tame ni* 199 (July 1990): 1-13.

Takahashi Yasuo et al., eds. *Zushū Nihon toshi shi*. Tokyo daigaku shuppan kai, 1993.

Takamure Itsue. *Nihon kon'in shi*. Jibun dō, 1963.

Takatori Masao. "Goryō shinkō o rikai suru tame ni." *Shisō* 38 (December 1980): 80-95.

Takeuchi Rizō. "Kodai no shūen." In *Kodai no Nihon 3 Kyushu*, edited by Kagamiyama Takeshi and Tamura Enchō, 354-61. Kadokawa shoten, 1970.

———. "Shōsōin koseki chōsa gaihō." *Shigaku zasshi* 68 (March 1959): 34-65.

Takigawa Masajirō. *Ritsuryō jidai no nōmin seikatsu*. Meichō fukyū kai, 1988.

Takinami Sadako. "Heian kyō no kōzō." In *Kodai o kangaeru Heian no miyako*, edited by Sasayama Haruo, 70-99. Yoshikawa kōbunkan, 1991.

A Tale of Flowering Fortunes. Translated by William and Helen McCullough. Stanford: Stanford University Press, 1980.

Tamura Noriyoshi. "Chusei jin no 'shi' to 'sei.'" *Nihonshi kenkyū* 388 (December 1994): 106-15.

Terauchi Takao. "Kōshoku jōri iseki Yashiro iseki gun ni miru saigai to kaihatsu." *Kokuritsu reikishi minzoku hakubutsu kan kenkyū hōkoku* 96 (March 2002): 23-52.

Toda Yoshimi. *Shoki chūsei shakai shi no kenkyū.* Tokyo daigaku shuppan kai, 1991.

———. "Jū-jūsan seiki no nōgyō rōdō to sonraku--aratauchi o chūshin toshite." In *Chūsei shakai no seiritsu to tenkai*, 309-31. Yoshikawa kōbunkan, 1976.

———. "Shōen taisei kakuritsu ki no shūkyōteki minshū undō." *Rekishigaku kenkyū* 378 (November 1971): 8-15.

———. *Nihon ryōshu sei seiritsu shi no kenkyū.* Iwanami shoten, 1967.

———. "Chūsei no hōken ryōshu sei." In *Iwanami kōza Nihon rekishi 6 Chūsei* 2, 218-60. Iwanami shoten, 1962.

Toire no kōkogaku. Tokyo bijutsu, 1997.

Tokunaga Chikako. "Shugendō seiritsu no shiteki zentei." *Shirin* 84 (January 2001): 97-123.

"Tokushū: kodai ni miru goryō to shinbutsu shūgō." *Kokubungaku: Kaishaku to kanshō* 36 (March 1999).

Tōno Haruyuki. "*Ko rissho zanpen* shikun." *Nanto bukkyō* 46 (1981): 83-102.

Tonomura, Hitomi. "Re-envisioning Women in the Post-Kamakura Age." In *The Origins of Japan's Medieval World*, edited by Jeffrey Mass, 138-69. Stanford: Stanford University Press, 1997.

———. "Black Hair and Red Trousers: Gendering the Flesh in Medieval Japan." *The American Historical Review* 99 (February 1994): 129-54.

Torao Toshiya. "Nara Economic and Social Institutions." In Vol. 1, *The Cambridge History of Japan*, edited by Delmer M. Brown, 415-52. Cambridge: Cambridge University Press, 1993.

Tosa Masahiko. "Nihon kodai seitetsu iseki ni kansuru kenkyū josetsu." *Tatara kenkyū* 24 (August 1981): 12-34.

Troost, Kristina. "Peasants, Elites, and Villages in the Fourteenth Century." In *The Origins of Japan's Medieval World*, edited by Jeffrey Mass, 91-109. Stanford: Stanford University Press, 1997.

Tsuchida Naoshige. *Nihon no rekishi 5 Ōchō no kizoku.* Chūō kōron sha, 1965.

Tsude Hiroshi. *Nihon nōkō shakai no seiritsu katei.* Iwanami shoten, 1989.

Tsuguda Yoshiharu. "Shōzui saii kō." *Senshū shigaku* 23 (April 1991): 50-71.

Tsunoyama Yukihiro. "Kodai no senshoku." In *Kōza Nihon gijutsu no shakai shi 3 Bōseki*, 7-35. Nihon hyōron sha, 1983.

Uejima Susumu. "Heian kōki kokka zaisei no kenkyū." *Nihonshi kenkyū* 360 (August 1992): 33-68.

———. "Jōkō sei no tenkai." *Shirin* 75 (July 1992): 74-113.

———. "Ikkoku heikin yaku no kakuritsu katei." *Shirin* 73 (January 1990): 41-72.

Umata Ayako. "Chūsei no hajimari." In *Aou shi shi*, 1:405-29, 710-718. Aou-shi kyōiku iinkai, 1984.

Uno Takao. *Shōen no kōkogaku.* Aoki shoten, 2001.

Urata Yoshie Akiko. "Henko sei no igi." *Shigaku zasshi* 81 (February 1972): 28-76.

Varley, Paul. *Warriors of Japan as Portrayed in the War Tales.* Honolulu: University of Hawai'i Press, 1994.

Wada Atsumu. "Nansan no kyūtō ryū." In *Nihon kokka no shiteki tokushitsu kodai chūsei*, 287-310. Shibunkaku shuppan, 1997.

Wakita Haruko. *Chūsei Kyoto to Gion matsuri.* Chūkō shinsho, 1999.

———. "Chūsei no kōtsū, un'yu." In *Kōza Nihon gijutsu no shakai shi* 8 *Kōtsū un'yu*, 101-42. Nihon hyōron sha, 1985.

Watanabe Makoto. "Heian chūki bōeki kanri no kihon kōzō." *Nihonshi kenkyū* 489 (May 2003): 31-50.

Winfield, Pamela. " Curing with *Kaji*: Healing and Esoteric Empowerment in Japan." *Japanese Journal of Religious Studies* 32 (2005): 107-30.

Yagi Hironori. *Suiden nōgyō no hatten ronri.* Nihon hyōron keizai sha, 1983.

Yamada Kunikazu. "'Zenki Heian-kyō' no fukugen." In *Toshi: Zenkindai toshi ron no shatei*, edited by Niki Hiroshi, 107-38. Aoki shoten, 2002.

Yamada Tatsuo. "Kinsei shōnōmin jiritsu no nōhōteki kiso." In *Nōhō tenkai no ronri*, 3-24. Ochanomizu shobō, 1975.

Yamamoto Kōji. "Tennō to shukusai." In *Iwanami kōza Tennō to ōken o kangaeru* 8 *Kosumorojii to shintai*, 153-76. Iwanami shoten, 2002.

Yamamoto Takashi. *Shōen sei no tenkai to chiiki shakai.* Tosui shobō, 1995.

Yamamoto Takeo. *Kikō no kataru Nihon rekishi.* Soshiete bunko, 1976.

———. "Rekishi no nagare ni sou Nihon to sono shūhen no kikō hensen." *Chigaku zasshi* 75 (March 1967): 119-41.

Yamamura, Kozo. "The Growth of Commerce." In Vol. 3, *The Cambridge History of Japan*, edited by Kozo Yamamura, 344-95. Cambridge: Cambridge University Press, 1990.

———. "The Decline of the *Ritsuryō* system: Hypotheses on Economic and Institutional Change." *Journal of Japanese Studies* 1 (autumn 1974): 1-37.

———. "The Development of *Za* in Medieval Japan." *Business History Review* 47 (winter 1973): 438-65.

Yamamura Shin'ei. "Chūsei Dazaifu no tenkai." In *Chusei toshi kenkyū* 4 *Toshi to shūkyō*, 65-86. Shin jinbutsu ōrai sha, 1997.

Yasuda Masahiko, "Heian-kyō no nioi." In *Kankyō rekishigaku no shiza*, edited by Hashimoto Yoshimasa, 135-160. Iwata shoin, 2002.

Yasuda Motohisa. *Nihon shoki hōken sei no kiso kenkyū*. Yamakawa shuppan, 1976.

Yi Hyŏn-suk. "7 segi Silla t'ongil chŏnchaeng gwa chŏnyombyŏng." *Yŏksa hwa hyŏnsil* 47 (March 2003): 117-47.

―――. "Silla t'ongilgi chŏnyombyŏng ui yuhaeng gwa taeŭngchaek." *Hanguk kodae sa yŏn'gu* 31 (September 2003): 209-56.

Yiengpruksawan, Mimi. *Hiraizumi*. Council on East Asian Studies, Harvard University, 1998.

―――. "The Visual Ideology of Buddhist Sculpture in the Late Heian Period as Configured by Epidemic and Disease." In *Iconography and Style in Buddhist Art Historical Studies*, 69-79. Kobe: Kobe University, 1995.

Yokoyama Sadahiro. "*Rissho zanpen* ni tsuite." *Kokushi kan daigaku kyōyō ronshū* 8 (March 1979): 1-20.

Yokoyama Yoshikiyo. "Honchō korai kokō kō." *Gakugei shirin* 5 (1879): 167-75.

Yoshida Takashi. *Taikei Nihon no rekishi 3 Kodai kokka no ayumi*. Shōgakkan, 1988.

―――. *Ritsuryō kokka to kodai no shakai*. Iwanami shoten, 1983.

―――. "Ritsuryō sei to sonraku." In *Iwanami kōza Nihon rekishi 3 Kodai 3*, 141-200. Iwanami shoten, 1976.

Yoshie Akiko. "Gender in Early Classical Japan." *Monumenta Nipponica* 60 (winter 2005): 437-79.

―――. *Nihon kodai no uji no kōzō*. Yoshikawa kōbunkan, 1986.

Yoshie Akira. "Kokufu kara yadomachi e." *Rekishi to bunka* 16 (1988): 118-68.

―――. "Chūsei zenki no kokufu." *Kokuritsu rekishi minzoku hakubutsukan kenkyū hōkoku*, 8 (December 1985): 23-101.

Yoshii Toshiyuki. "Yamato no kuni Ochi no kohori Ryōanji to goryō jinja." *Nihon shūkyō bunka shi kenkyū* 5 (2001): 113-41.

INDEX

Page numbers followed by f refer to figures; those followed by t refer to tables.

William Wayne Farris received his doctorate from Harvard University in 1981 and now holds the Sen Soshitsu XV Distinguished Chair in Japanese History and Culture at the University of Hawaii at Manoa. His research and writing have focused on the social and economic history of Japan to 1700, including such topics as disease and famine, agricultural technology and commerce, and aspects of the daily life of the common people. His major publications include *Population, Disease, and Land in Early Japan, 645-900* (Harvard University, 1985), *Heavenly Warriors: The Evolution of Japan's Military, 500-1300* (Harvard University, 1992), *Sacred Texts and Buried Treasures: Issues in the Historical Archaeology of Ancient Japan* (University of Hawaii, 1998), and *Japan's Medieval Population: Famine, Fertility, and Warfare in a Transformative Age* (University of Hawaii, 2006), which was named as an Outstanding Academic Title for 2006.

www.ingramcontent.com/pod-product-compliance
Lightning Source LLC
Chambersburg PA
CBHW020614270326
41927CB00005B/336